Martha Read

The National Cook Book

Ninth Edition

Martha Read

The National Cook Book
Ninth Edition

ISBN/EAN: 9783744763820

Printed in Europe, USA, Canada, Australia, Japan

Cover: Foto ©Andreas Hilbeck / pixelio.de

More available books at **www.hansebooks.com**

THE
NATIONAL COOK BOOK.

BY A

LADY OF PHILADELPHIA,

A PRACTICAL HOUSEWIFE.

A LADY IN WHOSE JUDGMENT WE HAVE THE MOST UNBOUNDED CONFIDENCE, PRONOUNCES THIS "THE ONLY COOK BOOK WORTHY OF A HOUSEKEEPER'S PERUSAL."
Graham's Magazine.

NINTH EDITION.

PHILADELPHIA:
GEORGE W. CHILDS, 628 & 630 CHESTNUT ST.
1863.

Entered according to the Act of Congress, in the year 1850, by
ROBERT E. PETERSON, in the Clerk's Office of the District
Court of the Eastern District of Pennsylvania.

DEACON & PETERSON, PRINTERS,
No. 66 S. Third Street.

The following pages, the result of long
experience, have been placed before the public, in
the hope that they may prove useful to all who
may consult them, and under the conviction that
they will be found truly practical.

The author has endeavored to draw them up in
the most concise and simple manner; and has in
all cases sacrificed *style* to minute detail; not even
avoiding repetition where it might render the directions more explicit.

A great defect in many works of a similar cha-
racter is, that the cook is forced to wade through a
formidable amount of reading before she can learn
the process of making a pudding, or discover the
different articles necessary to the concocting of a
dish.

Whilst some are so diffuse, others on the opposite extreme, are so brief in their explanations as
to fall far short of being understood, and consequently are ever liable to misconception.

As no utensils are requisite except those in common use in every family, the difficulty of preparing the various dishes will be greatly lessened.

Great attention has been paid to that department of cookery exclusively adapted to the sick or convalescent, most of the dishes having been prepared according to the directions of eminent physicians of Philadelphia.

Nearly all the receipts in this book are purely American; the author therefore entertains a hope that they may meet the wants of the community, and the approbation of all those who may honor them with a trial.

PHILADELPHIA, MAY, 1850.

CONTENTS.

SOUPS.

Beef,	15
Veal,	16
Pepper-pot,	17
Chicken,	18
Lamb,	18
Oyster,	19
Clam,	19
Green Corn,	19
Pea,	20
Succotash,	20
Noodles for,	20

FISH.

Rock, boiled,	21
fried,	22
Cod, boiled,	22
cakes,	23
Shad, spiced,	23
boiled,	23
fried,	24
broiled,	24
baked,	24
roasted on a board,	25
potted, No. 1,	25
No. 2,	26
Halibut,	26
Cat,	27
Potted herring,	27
Pickled oysters,	28
Fried oysters,	28
Stewed oysters, No. 1,	29
No. 2,	29
Scalloped oysters,	29
Oyster fritters,	30
pie,	30
Roasted oysters,	31
Oyster omelette,	31
Stewed clams,	32
Clam fritters,	32
Fried clams,	33
Terrapins,	33

Boiled crabs,	34
Soft crabs,	34
Boiled lobster,	35
Lobster salad,	35
Oyster omelette,	36

MEATS.

Beef, roast,	37
a-la-mode,	38
steaks,	38
steak, fried,	39
smothered,	39
baked and Yorkshire pudding,	39
French stew, No. 1,	40
No. 2,	41
Beef stewed with onions,	41
kidney, stewed,	41
fried,	42
corned,	42
Jewish method of preparing for salting,	43
boiled corned,	43
Boiled tongue,	43
Tripe,	43
Veal, roast,	44
pie, plain,	44
pot-pie,	45
fillet of, a-la-mode,	46
fillet of, baked,	46
French stew of,	47
stewed,	47
cutlets,	47
fried with tomatoes,	48
plain fried,	48
spiced,	48
Sweet-breads fried,	49
stewed,	49
boiled,	49
Calves' feet spiced,	49
fried,	50
liver fried,	50

CONTENTS.

Chitterlings, or Calves' tripe, - - - -	51
Lamb, roast leg of, -	51
boiled leg of, -	52
stewed with onions,	52
Mutton dressed like venison, - -	52
chops, - -	52
chops with lemon,	53
Pork, roast, - -	53
Pig, roast, - - - -	54
Pork, stuffed leg of, -	55
steaks, - - -	55
leg of, corned and boiled, - -	55
Spare rib, - . -	56
Soused pig's feet, - -	56
Scrapple, - - -	57
Hog's-head cheese, -	58
Boiled ham, - -	58
Glazed ham, - - -	59
Sausage meat, - -	59
Venison, to roast a haunch of, - -	59
steaks, - -	60
best way of cooking, - -	60
Rabbit, roasted, - -	61
pie, baked, -	61
pot-pie, - -	62
French stewed,	63
fricaseed, - -	63
smothered, -	64
Pigeons, roasted, - -	64
stewed, -	64
Squab, broiled, - -	65
Pigeon pie, - -	65
Reed Birds, stewed, No. 1,	65
No. 2,	66
roasted, -	67
pie, - -	67
fried, - -	67
Turkey, roasted, - -	68
boiled, - -	69
Duck, roasted, No. 1, -	69
No. 2, -	70
Goose, roasted, - -	70
Giblet pie, - - -	71
Chickens, roasted, -	72
pie, - -	72
pot-pie, -	73
Chickens, broiled, - -	73
fried, - -	74
boiled, -	74
stewed, -	75
Brown fricassee, - -	75
White fricasseed chicken,	76
Chicken salad, No. 1, -	76
No. 2, -	77

VEGETABLES.

Potatoes, boiled, No. 1, -	78
No. 2,	79
fried, No. 1, -	79
No. 2, -	80
No. 3, -	80
No. 4, -	80
Sweet Potatoes, fried, -	80
Potatoes, roasted, -	81
cakes, - -	81
kale, - -	81
salad, - -	82
sausage, -	83
Tomatoes, stewed, - -	83
fried, - -	83
baked, - -	84
scalloped, -	84
broiled, - -	84
dressed as cucumbers, -	85
fricandeau, -	85
Beets, baked, - -	85
Egg-plant, No. 1, -	86
No. 2, - -	86
No. 3, -	86
No. 4, - -	87
No. 5, - -	87
browned, -	88
Parsnips, No. 1, -	88
No. 2, - -	88
No. 3, -	88
No. 4, - -	89
stewed, -	89
Corn, boiled green, - -	89
fritters, - -	89
oysters, - -	90
Hominy, - - -	90
Sour krout, - -	91
boiled, - -	91
Cauliflower, - -	91
Slaw, cold, - -	92
hot, - .	92

CONTENTS.

Slaw, French,	92
Mushrooms,	93
Spinach,	93
as greens,	93
Dandelion,	94
Squashes or cymlins,	94
Ochrus,	94
Carrots,	95
Turnips,	95
Celery dressed as slaw,	95
stewed with lamb,	96
Asparagus,	96
Salad, Dutch,	96
corn,	97
Onions, boiled,	97
Cucumbers, fried,	98
Beans, Lima,	98
Windsor or horse,	98
stringed,	98
boiled dried,	99
Peas, green,	99
Salsify or oyster-plant, No. 1,	100
No. 2,	100
No. 3,	100
No. 4,	101

SAUCES.

Sauce, apple,	101
lemon,	101
Yorkshire,	102
nuns' butter,	102
dried peach,	102
cranberry,	103
wine,	103
rich wine,	103
cream,	104
vegetable,	104
tomato mustard,	105
egg,	105
drawn butter,	105
onion sauce,	106
mint,	106
mushroom,	106
parsley,	107
caper,	107
haslet,	107
horse-radish,	107
French tomato,	108
oyster,	108
tomato,	108

PICKLES.

Pickled peppers,	109
mushrooms, No. 1,	110
No. 2,	110
onions,	111
eggs,	111
Chow chow,	112
Pickled walnuts,	112
peaches,	113
beans,	113
mangoes,	114
cucumbers,	115
beets,	117
cherries,	117
Tomato catsup, No. 1,	117
No. 2,	118
Mushroom catsup,	119
Walnut "	119
Pickled nasturtiums,	119
tomatoes,	120

PASTRY.

Puff paste,	121
Plain "	122
Common paste,	122
Lemon pudding, No. 1,	122
No. 2,	123
Orange cheese-cake,	123
Lemon " "	124
Curd " "	125
Cottage " "	125
Indian florendines,	126
Rice "	126
Orange pudding,	127
Almond "	127
Cocoa-nut pudding, No. 1,	128
No. 2,	128
Apple pudding, No. 1,	129
No. 2,	130
Plain apple pudding, No. 3,	130
Pumpkin " No. 1,	131
No. 2,	131
Quince pudding,	132
French custard pudding,	133
Potato pudding,	133
Sweet potato pudding	134
Cranberry tarts,	134
Rhubarb tarts,	134
Ripe peach pie,	134

Peach pot-pie,	135
Quince pie,	135
Plum pie,	135
Quince dumplings,	136
Peach "	136
Apple "	136
Cherry pie,	137
Rhubarb pie,	137

SWEET DISHES.

Guernsey pudding,	137
Eve's "	138
French "	139
Sago "	139
French bread pudding,	140
Green corn "	141
Rice cup "	141
Newcastle "	141
Peach baked "	142
Farmer's apple "	142
Rice " No. 1,	143
No. 2,	143
Boiled rice "	144
Rice pudding, with fruit,	144
Rice cups,	144
Plum pudding,	145
Boiled " No. 1,	145
No. 2,	146
Indian boiled pudding,	146
baked "	147
Oxford pudding,	148
College "	149
Blanc mange,	150
Clear blanc mange,	150
Charlotte de Russe,	151
Peach Charlotte,	152
Savoy "	152
Cherry "	153
Rice milk,	153
Rice flummery,	154
Apple floating island,	154
Floating island,	155
Whips,	155
Syllabub,	156
Vanilla cup custard,	156
Hasty pudding, or farmer's rice,	156
Spanish fritters,	157
Apple "	157
Orange "	158

German puffs,	158
Snow custard,	159
Boiled custard,	159
Baked pears,	160
Stewed cherries,	160
Baked apples,	160
Blackberry mush,	160
Rice dumplings,	161
Glazed currants,	161
" strawberries,	162
Stewed ripe peaches,	162
Cold custard,	162
Apple cream,	163

TEA CAKES.

Short cake,	163
Muffins,	164
Hard biscuits,	164
Yorkshire biscuits,	165
Potato rolls,	165
Brentford rolls,	166
French "	166
Parsnip cake,	167
Maryland biscuits,	167
Waffles,	168
without yeast,	169
Buckwheat cakes,	169
Rye batter cakes,	170
Guernsey buns,	170
Tottenham muffins,	171
Crumpets, or flannel cakes,	171
Scotch crumpets,	172
Indian fritters,	172
Indian slappers,	173
pone,	174
Johnny or journey cake,	174
Indian light cake,	175
muffins, No. 1,	175
No. 2,	176
meal breakfast cakes,	176
Milk biscuits,	177
Sally Lunn, No. 1,	178
No. 2,	178
Water toast,	179
Milk "	179
Mush cakes,	179
Rice waffles,	180
Buttermilk cakes,	180
Indian Metland,	181
Cream-of-tartar cakes,	181

CAKES.

Fruit or plum cake, No. 1,	183
No. 2,	184
New York plum cake,	185
Pound-cake, No. 1,	186
No. 2,	187
Common pound-cake,	187
Cocoa-nut pound-cake,	188
Indian " "	189
Loaf cake,	189
Bristol loaf-cake,	190
Indian " "	191
Almond cake,	191
Sponge " No. 1,	192
" " No. 2,	193
" " No. 3,	193
Jumbles,	194
Spanish jumbles,	194
Plain "	195
Cocoa-nut "	195
Ginger fruit cake,	196
cup "	196
nuts,	197
bread, No 1,	198
No. 2,	198
Boston ginger-bread,	198
Common " "	199
Plain " "	199
Soda biscuit,	200
Kisses, or cream-cakes,	200
Sugar cake,	201
Federal "	202
White cup-cake,	202
German "	203
Seed cake,	203
Currant cake,	204
Rock "	204
Election "	205
Devonshire cakes,	205
Scotch cake,	206
Crullers,	206
Dutch loaf,	207
Rice cup-cake,	208
Cocoa-nut cakes,	208
Spanish buns,	209
Buns,	209
Dough-nuts,	210
Macaroons,	211
Lady cake,	211
Composition cake,	212

Scotch loaf,	213
French cake,	213
Travelers' biscuit,	215
Light sugar biscuits,	215
Plain cup-cake,	216
Apees,	217
Shrewsbury cake,	217
Dover biscuits,	218
Washington cake, No. 1,	218
No. 2,	219
Sugar biscuits,	220

PRESERVES.

Calf's-foot jelly,	222
Fox-grape "	222
Cranberry " No. 1,	223
" No. 2,	224
Orange "	224
Strawberry "	225
Currant "	225
Quince "	226
marmalade,	227
Peach "	227
Preserved pears,	227
quinces,	228
pine-apple,	228
peaches,	229
fresh figs,	230
citron melon,	230
green-gages,	231
plums,	232
Strawberry jam,	232
Cherry "	232
Raspberry "	233
Blackberry "	233
Green-gage "	233
Plum "	233
Pine-apple "	233
Brandy grapes,	233
peaches,	234

SICK.

Sago milk,	234
Orgeat,	235
Stewed prunes,	235
Cocoa,	235
Egg and wine,	236
Sago pudding, for invalids,	236
Tapioca pudding,	236

Arrow-root pudding, for invalids,	-	236
Pudding for the convalescent,	-	236
Indian gruel,	-	237
Egg and milk,	-	237
Sugared orange,	-	238
lemons, No. 1,		238
No. 2,	-	239
Mulled wine,	-	239
cider,	-	239
Vegetable soup,	-	240
Carrageen, or Irish moss,		240
Arrow-root,	-	241
Macaroni,	-	241
Lemonade, for an invalid,		241
Oat-meal gruel,	-	242
Baked pudding, for invalids,	-	242
Chicken broth,	-	242
Pap of unbolted flour,	-	243
grated "		243
Sweet-breads, for invalids,		243
Panada, No. 1,	-	244
No. 2,	-	244
Ground rice, No. 1,	-	245
No. 2,		245
Mustard whey,	-	245
Wine "	-	246
Vinegar "	-	246
Rennet "	-	246
Tamarind "	-	247
Potato jelly,	-	247
Port wine jelly,	-	247
Tapioca "	-	248
Hartshorn "	-	248
Rice "	-	248
Jelly of gelatine,	-	249
Slippery-elm tea,	-	249
Flax-seed "	-	250
Veal "	-	250
Beef "	-	250
Essence of beef,	-	251
Mutton tea,	-	251
Chicken "	-	251
Gum-arabic water,	-	251
Tamarind "	-	252
Grape "	-	252
Mulled "	-	252
Apple "	-	252
Barley "	-	253
Toast, water,	-	253
Almond "	-	253

MISCELLANEOUS.

Lemon Syrup, No. 1,	-	254
No. 2,	-	254
Ginger "	-	255
Brandy cherries	-	255
To preserve eggs during winter,	-	255
Blackberry cordial,	-	256
Raspberry brandy,	-	256
Currant shrub,	-	256
Raspberry shrub,	-	257
Cherry bounce,	-	257
Mixture for salting butter,		257
Egg-nog,	-	257
Minced meat,	-	258
Sandwiches,	-	259
Wine sangaree,	-	259
Porter "	-	259
Poached eggs,	-	260
Plain omelette,	-	260
Ham "	-	260
Bread "	-	261
Tomato "	-	261
Browned flour,	-	262
Dried cherries for pies,		262
apples "	-	263
peaches "	-	263
pumpkin "	-	263
To prepare saleratus,		264
Lemonade,	-	264
Punch,	-	264
Macaroni,	-	265
Indian mush,	-	265
Fried "	-	266
Welsh rabbit,	-	266
Mint julep,	-	266
Milk punch,	-	267
Cottage cheese,	-	267
To prepare rennet,	-	267
cure hams,	-	268
prepare apples for pies,		268
cure dried beef,	-	269
beef and hams,		269
shad,	-	270
roast coffee,		270
Coffee,	-	271
Chocolate,	-	271

CONTENTS.

Tea,	272
To make yeast,	272
Potato yeast,	273
Bread,	273
Potato bread,	274
Mush bread,	275
Rye "	275
Dyspeptic bread,	275
Fried "	275
Common mustard,	276
Icing for cakes,	276
To dry herbs,	276
Raspberry vinegar,	277
Celery "	277
Pepper "	277
Molasses candy,	278
Gooseberry pie,	278
Ripe currant pie,	279
Green "	279
Apple butter,	279
Jelly cake, No. 1,	280
No. 2,	281
Honey " No. 1,	282
No. 2,	282
Citron "	283
Vanilla kisses,	284
cake,	284
Ginger pound-cake,	285
Currant biscuits,	286
Plain crullers,	286
To make butter,	287
Queen cake,	288
Index,	291

TABLE

OF

WEIGHTS AND MEASURES.

For the convenience of those who have no scales and weights, the following table has been arranged. The measures correspond as nearly as possible with the weight of the different articles specified. These measures will answer for all the plainer cakes, &c but greater accuracy is necessary for the richer kinds.

AVOIRDUPOIS is the weight employed in this table.

Sixteen ounces	- -	are	- -	one pound.
Eight ounces	- -	are	- -	half a pound.
Four ounces	- -	are	- -	a quarter of a pound.

White sugar, (pulverized) four gills and a half, equal one pound.
Light brown sugar, three half pints, equal one pound.
    "   "   nine heaping table spoonsful, equal one pound.
Wheat flour, one quart and one table spoonful, equal one pound.
    "   fifteen heaping table spoonsful, equal one pound.
Ten eggs, equal one pound.
Fine Indian meal, one quart, equals one pound five ounces.
Coarse   "   one quart, equals one pound nine ounces.
Butter, one common sized tea-cup holds a quarter of a pound.
Spices, (ground) two large table spoonsful, equal one ounce.
Nutmegs, (whole) seven common sized, equal one ounce.

LIQUID MEASURE.

Two gills	- - -	are	- - -	half a pint.
Four gills	- - -	are	- - -	one pint.
Two pints	- - -	are	- - -	one quart.
Four quarts	- - -	are	- - -	one gallon.

Six common table spoonsful   - - -   equal one gill.
One wine glassful   - - - - -   equals half a gill.
One common sized tumblerful   - - -   equals half a pint.

THE NATIONAL COOK BOOK.

SOUPS.

All soups are better to be made with fresh uncooked meat, as that which has been cooked once has lost much of its flavor and nearly all its juices. It is therefore better economy to hash or spice your cold meat, and buy fresh for soup.

Soup should not boil *very* hard, as that has a tendency to toughen the meat.

Fat meat is not so proper nor healthy for soup as the leaner parts of the finest meat. The fat does not impart much flavor, and is not palatable.

Soup may be kept till the next day; before it is heated over again, skim off the cake of fat which congeals on the top. It is often preferred one day old to the day it is cooked.

BEEF SOUP.

1. Crack the bone of a shin of beef, and put it on to boil in one quart of water to every pound of meat, and a large tea spoonful of salt to each quart of water. Let it boil two hours, and skim it well. Then add four turnips pared and cut in quarters,

four onions pared and sliced, two carrots scraped and cut in slices, one root of celery cut in small pieces, and one bunch of sweet herbs; which should be washed and tied with a thread, as they are to be taken out when the soup is served. When the vegetables are tender, take out the meat, strain off the soup and return it to the pot again, thicken it with a little flour mixed with water; then add some parsley finely chopped, with more salt and pepper to the taste, and some dumplings, made of a tea spoonful of butter to two of flour, moistened with a little water or milk. Drop these dumplings into the boiling soup; let them boil five minutes and serve them with the soup in the tureen. Noodles may be substituted for the dumplings. For directions for making them see No 11.

VEAL SOUP.

2. Take a knuckle of veal, put it in a pot with four quarts of water, and add a tea spoonful of salt to each quart. Pare and slice three onions, four turnips, two carrots, a bunch of sweet herbs, and a small portion of celery. Let the veal boil one hour, then add the above vegetables. When they are tender, strain the soup. Put it in the pot it was boiled in, thicken the soup with some flour mixed smoothly with a little water, and add a little parsley finely chopped. Make some dumplings of a tea spoonful of butter to two of flour, and milk or

water enough to make a very soft dough. **Drop**
them into the boiling soup. They should be about
as large as a hickory-nut, when they are put in.
If noodles are preferred, they may be put in and
boiled ten minutes. For directions for making them
see No. 11. Dish the meat with the vegetables
around it. Drawn butter may be served with it,
or any other meat sauce.

PEPPER-POT.

3. Cut in small pieces four pounds of tripe,
put it on to boil in as much water as will cover it,
allowing a tea spoonful of salt to every quart of
water. Let it boil three hours, then have ready
four calves feet, which have been dressed with the
skin on. Put them into the pot with the tripe
and add as much water as will cover them; also
four onions sliced, and a small bunch of sweet herbs
chopped finely. Half an hour before the pepper-pot
is done add four potatoes cut in pieces; when these
are tender add two ounces of butter rolled in flour,
and season the soup highly with cayenne pepper.
Make some dumplings of **flour** and **butter** and **a
little water**—drop them into the soup; when **the
vegetables are sufficiently soft**, serve it.

The calves feet may be served with or without
drawn butter.

Any kind of spice may be added. If allspice **or
cloves** are used, the grains should be put in whole.

CHICKEN SOUP.

4. Wash a fine large chicken, put it in a pot and cover it with water with a little salt. Pick and wash two table spoonsful of rice, a bunch of sweet herbs, washed, and tied with a thread, two onions, and a little celery cut fine. Add these to the chicken as soon as it begins to boil. When the chicken is tender add a small bunch of parsley finely minced; let it boil a few minutes and then serve it. Season with pepper and salt to the taste. Serve the chicken with drawn butter. Some like allspice in this soup. If you should like it add a tea spoonful of the whole grains.

Noodles or dumplings may be substituted in place of the rice To make noodles see No. 11. The dumplings are made with a tea spoonful of butter, two of flour, and water enough to form a soft dough. Take a tea spoonful of the dough and drop into the boiling soup. Let them boil a few minutes.

Pearl barley may be used instead of rice.

LAMB SOUP.

5. Take a neck and breast of lamb, wash it, and to each pound of meat add a quart of water, and a tea spoonful of salt. Pare and slice two onions, two carrots, four turnips, two or three potatoes and a bunch of sweet herbs. Add all these to the meat after it has boiled one hour. If in the proper season add three or four tomatoes or half a dozen ochras.

When the vegetables are done, take out the meat, and add some flour mixed to a smooth paste with a little water. Noodles or dumplings may be added, as for beef soup. Some thicken lamb soup with a little rice put in the pot with the lamb.

OYSTER SOUP.

6. Take one hundred oysters out of the liquor. To half of the liquor add an equal quantity of water. Boil it with one tea spoonful of crushed allspice, a little mace, some cayenne pepper and salt. Let it boil twenty minutes, then strain it, put it back in the stew pan and add the oysters. As soon as it begins to boil, add a tea cupful of cream, and a little grated cracker rubbed in one ounce of butter. As soon as the oysters are plump, serve them.

CLAM SOUP.

7. Wash the shells of the clams and put them in a pot without any water. Cover the pot closely to keep in the steam; as soon as the clams are opened which will be in a few minutes, take them out of the shells and proceed as directed for oyster soup.

GREEN CORN SOUP.

8. Put on a knuckle of veal to boil in three quarts of water, and three tea spoonsful of salt. Cut the corn off of one dozen ears, and put it

on to boil with the veal. When the veal is tender the soup is done. Then roll an ounce of butter in flour and add to it before it is served. If the fire has been very hot and the water has boiled away too much, a little more may be added.

PEA SOUP.

9. This is made in the same manner as the green corn soup, only the peas must not be put in till about half an hour before the meat is done. A quart of peas will be requisite to make a dish of soup.

SUCCOTASH.

10. One quart of green corn cut off the cob, one quart of lima beans, and two pounds of pickled pork. If the pork should be very salt, soak it an hour before it is put on to boil. Put the pork on to boil and let it be about half cooked before the vegetables are put in. Then put in the corn (which must be cut off the cob) and the beans; let them boil till they are tender. Take all up, put the meat on a dish and the vegetables in a tureen. It should be a very thick soup when done.

TO MAKE NOODLES FOR SOUP.

11. Beat up an egg and to it add as much flour as will make a very stiff dough. Roll it out in a thin sheet, flour it, and roll it up closely, as you

would do a sheet of paper. Then with a sharp knife cut it in shavings about like cabbage for slaw; flour these cuttings to prevent them from adhering to each other, and add them to your soup whilst it is boiling. Let them boil ten minutes.

FISH.

Fish should always be perfectly fresh when cooked. To select fresh ones observe the eyes; if they have a bright life-like appearance the fish is fresh; if, on the contrary, the eyes are sunken and dark colored, and have lost their brilliancy, they are certainly stale. Some judge by the redness of the gills, but they are sometimes colored to deceive customers.

Crabs should be of a dark green color, and when fresh from the water are always very lively, the same remarks hold good with regard to lobsters. If the tail of the lobster will return to its former position when pulled out, the lobster is fresh.

Never buy a clam or oyster if the shells are parted. If the valves are tightly closed the oyster is fresh.

BOILED ROCK.

12. Scale a rock, take out the eyes and gills, draw it and wash it well. Flour a cloth, wrap the fish in it, and boil it in plenty of water strongly salted. A common sized fish requires about half

a large tea cupful of salt. Place your fish kettle over a strong fire, and when the water boils put in the fish. Let it boil hard twenty minutes. Take it out of the cloth carefully, place it on your fish dish and send it to the table. Have egg sauce in a sauce boat. Mashed potatoes are an accompaniment to boiled fish. Garnish the dish with green parsley.

If any of the boiled fish should be left from dinner it may be spiced as shad, and makes an excellent relish for breakfast or tea.

FRIED ROCK.

13. Clean and score your fish; wash and wipe them dry; season well with cayenne pepper and salt. Let them stand at least one hour before they are cooked, that the seasoning may have time to penetrate them. Have ready a pan of hot lard, dredge flour over your fish, put them in the pan and fry them slowly, that they may be done through. They should be of a handsome brown on both sides.

All pan fish are fried in the same way.

BOILED COD.

14. Soak a dried cod for three hours in cold water; scrape and wash it very clean; then put it on to boil in as much cold water as will cover it. Let it boil half an hour. Drain it on your fish dish,

and serve it with mashed potatoes, drawn butter, or egg sauce, and eggs boiled hard.

The castor should contain cayenne pepper, mustard, sweet oil, pepper, vinegar, and catsup.

COD FISH CAKES.

15. Boil a piece of salt cod; take out all the bones, and mash with it equal quantities of mashed potatoes. Season it with pepper and salt to your taste; then add as much beaten egg as will form it into a paste. Make it out into thin cakes, flour them and fry them of a light brown.

SPICED SHAD.

16. One large shad.
Two table spoonsful of salt.
Three tea spoonsful of cayenne pepper.
Two table spoonsful of whole allspice.
As much vinegar as will cover it.

Split the shad open, rub over it two table spoonsful of salt, and let it stand several hours. Have ready a pot with boiling water in it sufficient to cover the shad, allowing a tea spoonful of salt to every quart of water. Boil it twenty minutes. Take it out of the water, drain it, bruise your allspice just so as to crack the grains. Sprinkle over your shad the allspice and pepper, and cover it with cold vinegar.

BOILED SHAD.

17. Clean your shad, wash it and wipe it, flour it well, wrap it in a cloth, and put it into a large vessel of boiling water with a great deal of salt. It will require about twenty minutes to cook it. Serve it with egg sauce, or rich drawn butter.

FRIED SHAD.

18. Cut your shad in half, wash it and wipe it dry, score it and season with cayenne pepper and salt, dredge flour over it, and fry it in hot lard. When done, put the two halves together, that it may assume the appearance of a whole fish.

BROILED SHAD.

19. Split your shad down the back, wash it and season it well with salt. Have your gridiron heated, grease the bars, put on the shad and broil it slowly till quite done. It should be of a fine brown on both sides. If designed for the dinner table, after having basted it well with butter on both sides, fold it over, that it may assume its original form, and serve it.

BAKED SHAD.

20. Open your shad by cutting it down the back, wash it well and wipe it dry, score it and season it with cayenne pepper and salt; put it in a pan with two ounces of butter cut in small pieces,

put a few pieces of butter in the bottom of the pan and the remainder on the shad, add two table spoonsful of water. Place it in a very moderate oven and let it stand three or four hours.

SHAD ROASTED ON A BOARD.

21. Take a piece of clean oak board about three inches thick, and two feet square, stand it before the fire till the board is very hot, indeed almost charred. Have your shad split down the back, cleaned, washed, wiped dry, and seasoned with salt; fasten it to the hot board with a few small nails; the skin side should be next the board, place the board before the fire with the head part down; as soon as the juices begin to run, turn it with the tail down; it should be turned frequently in order to retain the juices. When done butter it and serve it hot. Send it to the table on the board.

This is the receipt for baking shad at the Philadelphia " fish house."

POTTED SHAD, No. 1.

22. Cut a shad in six or eight pieces, wash and wipe it dry. Mix one dessert spoonful of ground allspice, half a table spoonful of black pepper, and half a table spoonful of salt—sprinkle a portion of this seasoning over each piece of shad. Put them into a stone jar with enough good cider vinegar to cover them; cover the jar with a clean cloth, and

over this tie closely several thicknesses of brown paper to keep in the steam; set it in a moderate oven and let it remain twelve hours.

This is very good, but the fish is dark colored. When potted according to No. 2, it retains its whiteness.

POTTED SHAD, No. 2.

23. Cut a shad in about half a dozen pieces, wash it and wipe it dry. Mix together two table spoonsful of whole allspice and one table spoonful of whole black pepper; put one table spoonful and a half of salt over the shad the evening before it is to be potted, the next morning sprinkle over it a half a tea spoonful of cayenne pepper. Place the shad in a stone jar, and over each layer throw a portion of the grains of pepper and allspice, cover it with vinegar and set it in a moderate oven for twelve hours.

HALIBUT.

24. Cut it in slices about a quarter of an inch thick; wash and dry them, season with cayenne pepper and salt; have ready a pan of hot lard and fry your fish in it till of a delicate brown on both sides.

Some dip the cutlets in beaten egg and then in bread crumbs and fry it. When done in this manner it should be cut rather thinner than according to the first method.

Or, heat your gridiron, grease the bars, season your fish with cayenne pepper and salt, and broil it till of a fine brown color. Lay it on a dish and butter it.

CAT FISH.

25. Cut each fish in two parts, down the back and stomach; take out the upper part of the back bone next the head; wash and wipe them dry, season with cayenne pepper and salt, and dredge flour over them; fry them in hot lard of a nice light brown.

Some dress them like oysters; they are then dipped in beaten egg and bread crumbs and fried in hot lard. They are very nice dipped in beaten egg, without the crumbs, and fried.

POTTED HERRING.

26. Clean your herring, wash them well and wipe them dry; then rub each one with salt and cayenne pepper; place in your jar a layer of herring, then some grains of allspice, half a dozen cloves, and two or three blades of mace; then put in another layer of herring, and so on till all are in; cover the herring with cold vinegar, tie up the jar closely with several thicknesses of paper, and set it in the oven after the bread has been drawn out; let it remain there all night. As soon as they become cold they will be fit for use.

SHELL FISH.

PICKLED OYSTERS.

27. Take one hundred oysters out of their liquor, and add to them as much water as there was liquor. Put them over the fire, with salt to the taste, skim them, and as soon as they boil take them off. Have ready in a pan one gill of vinegar, one table spoonful of allspice, one table spoonful of pepper grains, a little cayenne pepper and mace, half a gill of pepper vinegar and half a gill of common vinegar. They should be pickled the day before they are to be eaten. After standing a few hours, if a scum should have risen on them, take out the oysters and strain the liquor. About six hours before they are to be served, slice a lemon and add to them

FRIED OYSTERS.

28. Select the largest oysters for frying. Take them out of their liquor with a fork, and endeavor in doing so, to rinse off all the particles of shell which may adhere to them. Dry them between napkins; have ready some grated cracker, seasoned with cayenne pepper and salt. Beat the yelks only of some eggs, and to each egg add half a table spoonful of thick cream. Dip the oysters, one at a time, first in the egg then in the cracker crumbs, and fry them in plenty of hot butter, or

butter and lard mixed, till they are of a light brown on both sides. Serve them hot.

STEWED OYSTERS, No. 1.

29. Take one hundred large oysters, add to them a quarter of a pound of butter, with salt, black and red pepper to the taste. Stew *as fast as possible* for three minutes. Serve them hot.

STEWED OYSTERS, No. 2.

30. Rinse one hundred oysters, and put them in a stew pan with the water which adheres to them; season them with salt and cayenne pepper, and a very little mace. As soon as they begin to boil pour in half a pint of cream, and stir in half an ounce of butter rolled in a little grated cracker. Let them boil once and serve them hot.

SCALLOPED OYSTERS.

31. Drain your oysters, and season them with salt and cayenne pepper; crumb some stale bread, and season it with salt and pepper. To each gill of the bread crumbs add one hard boiled egg, finely chopped; butter a deep dish, strew in a layer of egg and crumbs, then a layer of the oysters, with some lumps of butter on them, then more crumbs, and so on till all are in. Put a cover of crumbs on the top. Bake this in a tolerably quick oven and serve it hot.

OYSTER FRITTERS.

32. Drain the oysters and wipe them dry; season them with salt, if they are not salt enough; make a batter in the proportion of a pint of milk to three eggs, and flour to thicken it; beat the yelks till they are very thick, stir in the milk and as much flour as will make a batter, but not a very thick one; add a pinch of salt, beat the whole very hard, whisk the whites to a stiff dry froth and stir them in gently at the last. Put a small spoonful of the batter in a pan of boiling lard, then lay an oyster on the top, and over this put a little more batter; when they are brown on both sides, put them on a dish and send them to the table hot.

OYSTER PIE.

33. Take one hundred oysters out of their liquor, one at a time, so as to free them from any portions of the shell which might adhere to them. Drain and place them between clean napkins in order to dry them perfectly; pour off half the liquor into a stew-pan, salt it to your taste, stir in one gill of cream, one ounce and a half of butter rolled in grated cracker, and a little cayenne pepper; boil two eggs hard, chop them up, and mix them with as many bread crumbs as will cover the top of your pie; season the bread and egg with cayenne pepper and salt, make a rich paste, line the sides of

your pie dish, put in the oysters, pour the hot liquor over them, strew the bread crumbs on the top, cover the whole with a lid of paste, cut an opening in the centre of the top crust, and ornament it with flowers or leaves made of the paste, bake it and serve it hot. As soon as the crust is done take the pie out of the oven.

ROASTED OYSTERS.

34. Wash the shells perfectly clean, put them in pans and set them in the oven, or place them in rows on the top of your kitchen range. Those who live in the country, and have large wood fires, may roast them nicely on their hot hearth stone. Take them up as soon as the shells begin to open, before the liquor is lost; have ready a hot vegetable dish, take out the oysters and serve immediately. Or, the upper shell may be taken off, and the oysters placed on broad dishes in the other shell. The dishes must be well heated as the oysters should be eaten hot.

Each person dresses his oysters on his plate.

OYSTER OMELETTE.

35. Eight oysters chopped fine,
Six eggs,
A wine glassful of flour,
A little milk,
Pepper and salt to the taste.

Beat the eggs very light, add the oysters and the flour, which must be mixed to a paste with a little milk; pepper and salt to the taste. Fry it in hot butter, but do not turn it; as soon as it is done slip it on a dish and serve it hot.

The above is the usual mode of preparing oyster omelette; but the better way is to put your oysters in a stew pan, set them over the fire, and the moment they begin to boil take them out, drain them and dry them in a napkin. They are not so watery when prepared in this manner, and consequently will not dilute the beaten egg as much as the former mode. When they are cold mince them and proceed as above.

STEWED CLAMS.

36. Wash the clams, put them in a pot and cover them closely; set them near the fire, and as soon as they begin to open take them out of the shell; drain them, and to a pint of clams add half a pint of water, one ounce of butter rolled in flour, cayenne pepper and salt to the taste; let them stew ten minutes. Just before they are to be dished add one gill of cream.

CLAM FRITTERS.

37. Wash your clam shells, put them in a pot with the water only which adheres to them, cover the pot closely, and as soon as they open take them

out of the shell. Take out the hard part and cut the remainder in half, and season them with pepper and salt; beat the yelks of four eggs very light, add to them a pint of milk, a little salt, and flour enough to form a batter; whisk the whites very dry and add them at the last. Have ready a pan of hot lard, put in a spoonful of the batter, lay on the top two or three pieces of the clams, then cover them with a little more of the batter. Fry them on both sides and serve them hot.

The small sand clams are the best kind.

FRIED CLAMS.

38. Wash your clams before they are opened; place them in a vessel without any water. Cover the vessel closely and as soon as they open their mouths take them out of the shell. Dry them in a napkin, season them with cayenne pepper and salt if necessary, and fry them in butter. Or, they may be fried in egg and bread crumbs as oysters.

TERRAPINS.

39. Put the terrapins on in boiling water and let them boil ten minutes, take them out and with a coarse cloth rub all the skin off the head, neck, and claws, also the thin shell that may come loose. Then boil them in clean water, with a little salt in it, until the claws are perfectly soft. The time of boiling depends very much on the age of the terra-

pin; some take three hours. When they are soft, open them carefully, take out the sand bag, the spongy part, and the gall, which you must not break. Cut all the remainder of the terrapin in small pieces, put them in a stew pan, and to each large terrapin take a quarter of a pound of butter, one wine glass of Sherry or Madeira wine, salt, black and red pepper, and mustard, to suit the taste, also to each terrapin, the yelks of two hard boiled eggs, mashed to a paste, with a little butter. Mix the whole together, and stew fifteen minutes. Send them to the table hot.

BOILED CRABS.

40. Have a large pot of water strongly salted, let it boil hard, put in your crabs and boil them for twenty minutes. If the water should cease boiling the crabs will be watery. Take them out, break off the claws, wipe the shells very clean, also the large claws

When cold, place them on a dish with the large claws around it. The claws should be cracked before they are sent to the table. The small ones are not generally eaten.

SOFT CRABS.

41. Prepare your crabs by removing the spongy part, and sand bag. Wipe them very clean and fry them in some hot lard and butter mixed. When

they are a fine yellow brown on both sides, place them on a dish and send them to the table hot.

BOILED LOBSTER.

42. Lobsters, as well as crabs, should be boiled in strong salt and water. Have your pot of water boiling hard, put in your lobsters and boil them for half an hour, or if they are very large, a little longer. Take them out of the pot and when they have drained, open them, extract the meat carefully, and send it to the table cold.

Lobster is usually dressed at the table with mustard, hard boiled eggs, cayenne pepper, salt, vinegar and oil.

LOBSTER SALAD.

43. One large lobster.
Three table spoonsful of French mustard, or,
Two dessert spoonsful of common mixed mustard.
One gill and a half of vinegar.
One gill and a half of sweet oil.
The yelks of five hard boiled eggs.
Salt to the taste.
A small tea spoonful of cayenne pepper.
The inside leaves of two heads of cabbage lettuce.

Cut the meat and lettuce in small pieces. Boil the eggs hard, mash the yelks with a wooden or silver spoon, and oil enough to make them to a smooth paste, then add the vinegar, mustard, pepper, and salt to the taste. Mix this dressing thoroughly with the lobster and lettuce, and serve it before the salad becomes wilted.

OYSTER OMELETTE.

44. Beat four eggs very light. Cut the hard part out of eight or a dozen oysters, according to their size, wipe them dry, and cut them up in small pieces, stir them into the beaten egg and fry them in hot butter. When the under side is brown, sprinkle a little salt and pepper over the top, and fold one half over the other.

Never turn an omelette, as it makes it heavy.

MEATS.

The finest grained beef is the best, the flesh is of a fine red, and the fat a light cream color, but not yellow; the fat, too, is solid and firm. The lean of mutton should be of a red color, and the fat white. The lean of veal should be of a light color and the fat white. The skin of pork should be of a light color, and if young it is tender. The fat should appear firm. A tender goose is known by taking hold of the wing and raising it; if the skin tears easily, the goose is tender, or if you can readily insert the head of a pin into the flesh, it is young. The same remarks will hold good with regard to ducks. Young chickens may be known by pressing the lower end of the breast bone; if it yields readily to the pressure they are not old, for in all animals the bones are cartilaginous when young. The breast should be broad and plump in all kinds of poultry, the feet pliable, and the toes easily broken when bent back.

ROAST BEEF.

45. The nicest piece for roasting is the rib.

Two ribs of fine beef is a piece large enough for a family of eight or ten. The lean of beef should always appear of a bright red before it is cooked, and the fat of a very light cream color.

Season the beef with salt, and place it in a roaster before a clear bright fire. Do not set it too close at first. As to the time of roasting, that must be left to the judgment of the cook and the taste of those who are to eat it. If it is preferred quite rare an hour and a half or two hours will cook two large ribs sufficiently, but if it is to be better done, it must be cooked a proportionably longer time. Whilst the beef is roasting, baste it frequently with its own gravy. When nearly done, dredge flour lightly over it so as to brown it. When the meat is taken out, skim off the fat on the top of the gravy, and pour the remainder in a pan, add a little flour, with salt to the taste, and some water, give it one boil, and serve it in a small tureen or gravy boat.

In cold weather the plates should be warmed just before the dinner is served. Or, a small chafing dish placed under each plate.

BEEF A-LA-MODE.

46. A round of beef is the best for this purpose. With a sharp knife cut incisions in the meat about an inch apart, and within one inch of the opposite side, season it with pepper and salt according to the size of the piece of meat.

Make a dressing of butter, onion, and bread crumbs, in the proportion of a pint of crumbs, one small onion finely chopped, and an ounce of butter, with pepper and salt to the taste, fill the incisions with the dressing, put the meat in a pot, with about a pint of water, and cover it tightly. Let it simmer six or eight hours.

Some stick in a few cloves, and those who are fond of spice add allspice. When the meat is done, dish it up and thicken the gravy with a little flour. Let it boil once, and serve it. This is excellent when cold.

BEEF STEAKS.

47. Scrape some fine sirloin steaks, wipe them with a clean cloth, heat the bars of your gridiron, grease them, and put your steaks over clear coals

Turn them frequently by placing a dish over them, and then quickly turn them, holding the dish in one hand and the gridiron in the other. In this manner you will preserve the gravy. When done, season them with pepper and salt; baste them well with butter, and add two table spoonsful of water, with a little salt. Send them to the table hot.

FRIED BEEF STEAK.

48. Season your steaks with salt and pepper, and fry them in hot lard. When done, dish them, add a little flour to the fat they were fried in, pour in a little water, and season with pepper and salt to the taste; give the gravy one boil and pour it over.

SMOTHERED STEAK.

49. Take one dozen large onions, boil them in very little water until they are tender.

Pound and wash a beef steak, season it with pepper and salt, put it in a pan with some hot beef dripping, and fry it till it is done. Take it out, put it on a dish, where it will keep hot. Then, when the onions are soft, drain and mash them in the pan with the steak gravy, and add pepper and salt to the taste. Put it on the fire and as soon as it is hot, pour it over the steak and serve it.

BAKED BEEF, AND YORKSHIRE PUDDING.

50. Rub salt on a nice piece of beef, put it on bars, which should fit your dripping pan, set it in

the oven, with a gill of water in the pan, and when it is half done, make the pudding in the following manner:

Beat four eggs very light; the yelks in a pan, the whites in a broad dish. When the yelks are thick stir in a pint of milk, and as much flour as will make a batter, but not a thick one. Then stir in the whites which must be whisked very dry;.do not beat the batter after the white is in; lastly stir in a tea spoonful of dissolved carbonate of ammonia. Take out the meat, skim all the fat off the gravy, pour in the batter and replace the meat; put all into the oven again, and cook it till the pudding is done. You should make batter enough to cover your dripping pan about half an inch deep. When the meat is dished, cut the pudding in squares, and place it round the dish, the brown side up.

FRENCH STEW, No 1.

51. Cut up two pounds of beef, and add to it a pint of sliced tomatoes. The tomatoes must be peeled. Put the meat in a stew-pan and season it well with pepper and salt, then add your tomatoes and an ounce of butter rolled in flour. Cover it closely, and let it simmer till the beef is tender. It does not require any water as the tomatoes are sufficiently juicy.

If the gravy should not be thick enough, add a little flour mixed with cold water.

FRENCH STEW, No. 2.

52. Cut up one pound of beef in small pieces about an inch square, pare and slice six onions; put a layer of the meat and a layer of onions in a stew-pan, with salt and pepper and a little flour alternately till all is in, and add half a tea cupful of water; cover it closely and set it on a slow fire to stew; when about half done, if the gravy seems too thin, add one ounce of butter rolled in flour; but if it should be thick enough, add the butter without the flour.

When tomatoes are in season two tomatoes may be cut in small pieces and stewed with the meat

Cold beef may be cooked in the same manner.

BEEF STEWED WITH ONIONS.

53. Cut some tender beef in small pieces, and season it with pepper and salt, slice some onions and add to it, with water enough in the stew-pan to make a gravy; let it stew slowly till the beef is thoroughly done, then add some pieces of butter rolled in flour to make a rich gravy.

Cold beef may be done in the same way, only the onions must be stewed first and the meat added. If the water should stew away too much put in a little more.

STEWED BEEF'S KIDNEY.

54. Clear the kidney of all the fat, cut it in two,

and with a sharp knife cut out the fibre which runs through the middle of it. Lay it in a sauce-pan with a very little water and a little salt, cover it close and let it stew till it is perfectly tender, then take it up and cut it in small pieces, season it with pepper, and more salt if requisite, and return it to the stew-pan; let it stew till there are about two spoonsful of gravy remaining in the stew-pan, then add a piece of butter and a little flour. Let it boil once and serve it.

FRIED BEEF'S KIDNEY.

55. Clean all the fat off the kidney, cut it open and take out the fibre which runs through it; put it in a stew-pan with a very little water and some salt, and cook it till it is tender; then season it with pepper and more salt if required, flour it and fry it in hot lard, add a little flour and water to make the gravy.

Or, you may broil instead of frying it, after it has been parboiled.

CORNED BEEF.

56. One hundred pounds of beef,
Six pounds of coarse salt,
Two ounces and a half of saltpetre,
One pound and a half of sugar,
Four gallons of water.

Mix the above ingredients together and pour over the meat. Cover the tub closely.

JEWISH METHOD OF PREPARING BEEF FOR SALTING.

57. Take out all the veins. Sprinkle with salt and let it lay for half an hour; wash off all the salt and soak it half an hour in cold water, drain it and then put it in the pickle as directed above.

BOILED CORNED BEEF.

58. Put on the meat in cold water; allow one quart of water to every pound of meat. The slower it boils the better it will be. For every pound of meat let it boil fifteen minutes; thus, a piece of beef weighing twelve pounds should boil three hours. If the beef is to be eaten cold—as soon as it is taken out of the pot immerse it in cold water for a short time, in order to retain the juices.

Tongues are boiled in the same manner.

BOILED TONGUE.

59. See boiled corned beef, Article 58.

TRIPE.

60. Scrape and wash it very clean—put it in a

pot with a tea spoonful of salt to every quart of water, and let it boil till the top of each piece begins to look clear—it requires a great deal of boiling and must be exceedingly soft.

When cold cut it in pieces, season and fry it in egg and bread crumbs like oysters. Or, it may be fried without the egg and crumbs, and the gravy thickened with a little flour, and flavored with catsup or vinegar. Serve it hot.

ROAST VEAL.

61. Season a breast of veal with pepper and salt; skewer the sweet-bread firmly in its place, flour the meat and roast it slowly before a moderate fire for about four hours—it should be of a fine brown but not dry; baste it with butter. When done put the gravy in a stew-pan, add a piece of butter rolled in browned flour, and if there should not be quite enough gravy add a little more water, with pepper and salt to the taste. The gravy should be brown.

PLAIN VEAL PIE.

62. Take the best end of a neck of veal, cut it in pieces, season it with pepper and salt, and stew it in just enough water to cover it. When it is nearly done make a rich gravy with some butter rolled in flour, added to the water it was stewed in.

Line the sides of a deep pie dish with paste, put in the meat and pour in the gravy, roll out a sheet of paste and cover the top; cut an opening in the centre of the top, about three inches long, and another to cross it at right angles; turn back the four corners and ornament with bars of paste twisted and laid over. Set it in the oven, and when the crust is done send it to the table in the dish it was baked in.

VEAL POT PIE.

63. Cut up some veal, the best part of the neck is preferable to any other, wash and season it with pepper and salt; line the sides of your pot with paste, put in the veal with some pieces of paste rolled out and cut in squares, cut up some pieces of butter rolled in flour and add to it, pour in as much water as will cover it, and lay a sheet of paste on the top, leaving an opening in the centre; put the lid on the pot and put it over a moderate fire, let it cook slowly till the meat is done; place the soft crust on a dish, then put the meat over it, and on the top lay the hard crust, with the brown side up. Serve the gravy in a boat.

To have the crust of a pot pie brown, set the pot on a few coals before the fire, and turn it frequently.

FILLET OF VEAL A-LA-MODE.

64. Cut deep incisions in the meat about an inch apart, and season it with pepper and salt. Make your dressing with a four cent baker's loaf, two small onions finely chopped, and an ounce of butter, with pepper and salt to the taste; fill the incisions with this dressing, put the veal in a pot with three gills of water and cover it tightly. Let it cook slowly two hours at least. Some prefer a little sweet marjoram or thyme, finely powdered, added to the dressing. Take out the veal when it is done, and thicken the gravy with a little flour.

BAKED FILLET OF VEAL.

65. Make incisions all around the bone as closely as possible, so as not to touch each other. Make a dressing of bread crumbs, an onion finely chopped, a little sweet marjoram, pepper and salt to the taste, with enough butter to cause the bread crumbs to adhere together; fill these incisions with the dressing, season the meat with pepper and salt, and skewer the strip of fat around it. Pour in enough water to cover the bottom of the pan, put in the rack and place the meat on it; as the gravy stews away add a little more water, put it in a cool oven and let it cook three or four hours. When done, make the gravy with some flour rolled in butter, and add pepper and salt to the taste.

FRENCH STEW OF VEAL.

66. Boil a knuckle of veal in just enough water to cover it, with a little salt. When the veal is tender pour off the water it was boiled in and save it. Cut the veal in small pieces and put it in a pan with the water it was boiled in. Add to this two hard boiled eggs, chopped very fine, a table spoonful of allspice in grains, (which should be crushed but not broken fine) a quarter of a pound of butter, a little mace and pepper, and salt to the taste. Stir two table spoonsful of flour smoothly in a little water, and pour into it. Set it over the fire, let it boil for two or three minutes, pour in two glasses of wine, and serve it hot.

STEWED VEAL.

67. Cut a slice of the cutlet in small pieces, season it with pepper, salt, and, if you prefer it, a little grated lemon peel and nutmeg. Pour in as much water as will nearly cover it, let it cook slowly till about half done, then make a rich gravy with some pieces of butter rolled in flour, and add to the water it was stewed in.

VEAL CUTLETS.

68. Cut the veal in thin slices, pound and wash it, then dry it in a clean cloth. Beat some egg, and have ready some bread crumbs, or grated cracker. Season the meat with salt, pepper, and a

little mace, dip each slice in the egg, then in the crumbs, and fry them in hot lard. They should be brown on both sides.

FRIED VEAL WITH TOMATOES.

69. Cut some veal in thin slices, season it and fry it of a nice brown. Have ready some tomatoes which have been stewed very dry; pass them through a seive to take out the seeds. Then put them into the pan in which the meat has been fried and add butter enough to make a rich gravy. Pour them hot over the veal and serve it.

Beef is excellent cooked in the same way.

PLAIN FRIED VEAL.

70. Cut the meat in thin slices, pound and wash them. Season with pepper and salt, and fry them in hot lard, of a nice brown, on both sides. When the meat is done stir a little flour into the fat and pour in some water; set the pan over the fire, let it boil once, then pour it over the veal, and send it to the table.

SPICED VEAL.

71. Take some of the thick part of a cold loin of veal, cut it in small pieces, and pour over as much hot spiced vinegar as will cover it.

To half a pint of vinegar put a tea spoonful of

allspice, a very little mace, salt and cayenne pepper to the taste.

FRIED SWEET-BREADS.

72. Parboil them in salt and water; when done, take them up and dry them in a cloth. With a sharp knife, cut them in half, season them with pepper and salt, and flour them, fry them in hot lard, of a light brown. Or they may be fried as oysters, with egg and bread crumbs, or grated crackers.

STEWED SWEET-BREADS.

73. Put them on in very little water with some salt, when they have cooked slowly for half an hour, take them out. Cut them in small pieces, and return them to the liquor they were boiled in. Make a rich gravy of butter rolled in flour, and pepper and salt to the taste. Mace and nutmeg may be added if preferred.

BOILED SWEET-BREADS.

74. Wash and dry them, and rub them with dry flour and a little salt, then put them in a stew-pan, with water sufficient to keep them from burning. When they are tender, put them in a dish and pour over a rich drawn butter.

SPICED CALVES' FEET.

75. Boil them as directed for fried calves' feet

in the following receipt, and save the liquor they were boiled in. When cold, cut them in pieces, and put them in a jar; take equal portions of the liquor they were boiled in, and good sharp vinegar; to every pint of this mixture add a tea spoonful of allspice crushed, two or three blades of mace, and salt and cayenne pepper to the taste. Heat the vinegar, liquor, and spices together, and pour it hot over the feet.

This makes a good dish for tea or breakfast.

FRIED CALVES' FEET.

76. Boil them in very little water, with some salt. There should be no more water than barely sufficient to cook them. When they are tender, cut them in half, and place them on a dish to get cold. Save the liquor they were boiled in. When they are to be fried season them with pepper and salt, dredge flour over them and fry them in hot lard or butter.

They should be of a handsome brown on both sides when done. Put some of the liquor they were boiled in, in the pan, and make a rich gravy with some pieces of butter rolled in flour. Pour this over the fried feet, and send them to the table.

FRIED CALVES' LIVER.

77. Cut the liver in thin slices and lay them in salt and water for several hours, to draw out all

the blood. Then season them with pepper and salt, and fry them in hot lard. When they are done, thicken the gravy with a little flour, and add a little water. Let it boil once, pour it over the liver, and serve it.

It should be fried slowly, or it will be brown on the outside before it is done through. Some prefer the liver fried without any gravy made for it. In that case, lay the slices on the dish and serve.

It may be broiled and buttered.

CHITTERLINGS, OR CALVES' TRIPE.

78. Wash them and put them on to boil in water enough to cover them, with a little salt. When they are quite tender, drain them, put them on a dish, and pour over them a rich drawn butter.

ROAST LEG OF LAMB.

79. Cut deep incisions round the bone and in the flesh; make a dressing of bread crumbs, salt, pepper, sweet marjoram, or summer savory, and as much butter as will make the crumbs adhere together. Fill all the incisions with the dressing, season the meat with salt and pepper, put it on the spit and roast it before a clear fire; when nearly done dredge flour over and baste it with the gravy.

Skim the fat off the gravy, and add a little flour, mixed with water; let it boil once, and serve it in a gravy boat.

BOILED LEG OF LAMB.

80. Trim off all the loose fat, cut off the shank, wash and wipe it dry; dredge it with flour and tie it in a clean cloth; put it in boiling water enough to cover it. The water should be salted in the proportion of two tea spoonsful of salt to a quart of water. Let it boil from two to three hours according to its size. Serve it with drawn butter or rich parsley sauce, which ever may be preferred, and vegetables of any kind which may be in season.

LAMB STEWED WITH ONIONS.

81. This is a French dish. Peel some onions, cut them in slices, and put them in your stew-pan; cut off the ends of the chops, pound them, and lay them in with the onions and some pepper and salt. Put in as much water as will cook them; let them stew slowly till they are tender, then add a piece of butter rolled in flour to thicken the gravy.

MUTTON DRESSED LIKE VENISON.

82. Hang a leg of mutton and let it freeze. Then cut from it slices about a quarter of an inch thick, cook them at the table in a chafing dish with butter and currant jelly, and salt and pepper to the taste.

MUTTON CHOPS.

83. Trim your mutton chops, take off the loose

fat, and heat your gridiron; grease the bars, put on the chops over clear coals, turn them frequently, and when done put them in a dish, butter them well and season with pepper and salt.

They may be served with slices of lemon.

MUTTON CHOPS WITH LEMON.

84. Wash the chops, wipe them dry, grease the bars of your gridiron, and broil them over hot coals. When they are done lay them on a dish and season them with pepper and salt, and baste them with butter; peel and slice lemons, lay a slice on each chop and send them to the table.

This is the French method of serving them.

ROAST PORK.

85. Take a nice middle piece of young pork, separate the joints and crack the bones across the middle, but do not break the skin, score it parallel with the ribs, wash it, put it on the spit, with a little water in the bottom of the roaster, and to five pounds of pork rub in well two tea spoonsful and a half of salt, two tea spoonsful of sage and one of cayenne pepper. Put no flour on it nor baste it while cooking, as it softens the skin and makes it tough. Pour the gravy into a pan, skim off a part of the fat, stir in a little flour mixed with cold water, add some water and let it boil once, then

serve it in a gravy tureen. If it should not be sufficiently seasoned, add a little more pepper or salt, as it may require.

Apple sauce is always served with roast pork.

ROAST PIG.

86. Prepare the pig by cutting off the feet, scraping and cleansing the head and ears, cutting out the tongue and eyes, and cleaning the throat. Wash it perfectly clean and wipe it dry. Make a dressing of bread crumbs, some onions finely chopped, with salt, pepper, and sweet marjoram to the taste, also butter enough to make the crumbs adhere together. Any spice may be added, and the grating of a lemon, but many prefer the dressing without spice.

Rub the pig thoroughly inside with salt, cayenne pepper, and powdered sage, then fill it with the dressing and sew it up. Rub the outside with salt, cayenne pepper and sage, put it on the spit and place it before a clear, but not too hot a fire. Have a piece of clean sponge tied on a stick, dip it in melted butter, and as the skin dries moisten it. A common sized pig takes from three to four hours to roast. An excellent filling may be made of potatoes boiled and mashed instead of the bread. If potatoes are used the dressing will require more butter.

Roast pig is always served with haslet sauce.

For directions for making it see under the head of Sauces. Apple sauce is also thought to be an indispensable accompaniment to roast pig.

STUFFED LEG OF PORK.

87. Make deep incisions in the meat parallel to the bone; trim it so as to leave the skin longer than the flesh; then boil some potatoes, when they are done mash them with a piece of butter, cayenne pepper, salt, and an onion finely chopped and a little rubbed sage. With this dressing fill the incisions, draw the skin down and skewer it over to keep the dressing from falling out; season the outside of the meat with salt, cayenne pepper, and rubbed sage; roast it slowly; when it is done pour the gravy in a pan, skim off the fat, and add a little flour mixed with water; let it boil once. Serve it with apple or cranberry sauce. Some prefer a dressing made of bread crumbs instead of potatoes.

PORK STEAKS.

88. Cut the steaks in thin slices, season them with cayenne pepper, salt, and rubbed sage. They may be broiled and buttered, or fried in hot lard, with a gravy thickened with a little flour and poured over them.

LEG OF PORK CORNED AND BOILED.

89. Mix salt and sugar together, in the proportion

of a table spoonful of salt to one tea spoonful of sugar; with this mixture rub your meat all over well, let it stand three days, and turn it every day. Have boiling water enough to cover it, put in the meat, and if the water should boil away put more in; when it is tender, serve it with tomatoes, cabbage, turnips, or any vegetables in season.

SPARE RIB.

90. Crack the ribs across, separate the joints, wash it and season it with cayenne pepper, salt, and rubbed sage; put it on the spit and cook it slowly till it is done. This is served without gravy.

Or, it may be prepared in the same manner and broiled on the gridiron.

SOUSED PIG'S FEET.

91. After they have been well scalded and cleaned, wash them, and put them on to boil in a sufficiency of water to cover them, with two tea spoonsful of salt to a quart of water. Let them boil till the bones are all loose and the flesh nearly ready to fall to pieces. Take them out and lay them on a dish to get cold, and save the liquor they were boiled in; mix equal portions of the liquor and good sharp vinegar, with whole allspice, a few cloves, pepper and salt to the taste. Heat the vinegar and spice, and pour it over them. They may

be sent to the table cold, or they may be heated with a portion of the vinegar.

The feet may be boiled as for the souse, and when cold, cut in half, dredged with flour, and fried brown.

SCRAPPLE.

92. This is generally made of the head, feet, and any pieces which may be left after having made sausage meat.

Scrape and wash well all the pieces designed for the scrapple, put them in a pot with just as much water as will cover them. Add a little salt, and let them boil slowly till the flesh is perfectly soft, and the bones loose. Take all the meat out of the pot, pick out the bones, cut it up fine, and return it to the liquor in the pot. Season it with pepper, salt, and rubbed sage, to the taste. Set the pot over the fire, and just before it begins to boil, stir in gradually as much Indian meal as will make it as thick as thick mush. Let it boil a few minutes, take it off, and pour it in pans. When cold, cut it in slices, flour it, and fry it in hot lard, or sausage fat.

Some prefer buckwheat meal; this is added in the same manner as the Indian. Indian meal is preferable, as it is not so solid as buckwheat.

Sweet marjoram may be added with the sage, if preferred.

HOGS-HEAD CHEESE.

93. Clean a pig's head nicely, wash it well, and boil it in very little water, with some salt. Let it boil until the bones fall from the flesh. Then take it up, pick out all the bones, and with a wooden spoon mash it up well, and return it to the water it was boiled in. Add red and black pepper, rubbed sage and sweet marjoram to the taste. Boil the whole down till it is quite thick and nearly dry; then pour it in pans or forms, smooth it over the top with the back of a spoon, and stand it away to get cold. Cut it in slices and send it to the table.

Some prefer spice in hogs-head cheese; in that case, add a small quantity of ground cloves and mace.

BOILED HAM.

94. Wash and scrape your ham; if it is not very salt it need not be soaked; if old and dry, let it soak twelve hours in lukewarm water, which should be changed several times. Put it in a large vessel filled with cold water. Let it simmer, but be careful not to let it boil, as it hardens and toughens the meat. Allow twenty minutes to cook each pound of meat.

When it is done, take it out of the water, strip off the skin, and serve it. Twist scalloped letter paper round the shank, or ornament it with sprigs of green parsley neatly twisted round it. If it is not to be eaten whilst hot, as soon as it is taken from the pot, set it away to get cold, then skin it, by which means you preserve all the juices of the meat. It may be garnished as above, or, if you choose, you may glaze it; the receipt for which see under its proper head.

GLAZED HAM.

95. Beat the yelks of two eggs very light, cover your ham all over with the beaten egg, then sift over some grated cracker, and set the ham in the oven to brown the glazing.

SAUSAGE MEAT.

96. Twenty-five pounds of pork.
Half a pint of salt.
One gill of rubbed sage.
Half a gill of black pepper.
One table spoonful of cayenne pepper.

TO ROAST A HAUNCH OF VENISON.

97. Put your venison on a spit before a clear, steady fire, cover it with some thick paper to keep it from burning, and place it at a sufficient distance from the fire, that it may not brown too soon. The paper may be fastened on by sticking through it two or three large darning needles. Turn the spit frequently, and baste the meat with butter. Venison is very unpalatable if too much cooked; about

two hours will be sufficient. It should never be roasted unless it is fat. A gravy may be made of the trimmings of the haunch stewed in very little water, to which add the drippings from the meat, season with pepper and salt, and thicken with butter rolled in flour.

Some baste with melted butter and wine mixed together. Serve with currant jelly.

VENISON STEAKS.

98. Cut your venison in slices, pound it, and having heated your gridiron, grease the bars and place the meat on it. Broil the venison very quickly over clear coals, and as soon as it is done put it on a dish, season with pepper and salt and plenty of butter. Send it to the table immediately. Serve it with currant jelly. The plates should be warm.

BEST WAY OF COOKING VENISON.

99. Cut your venison in rather thin slices, pound them, lay them on a dish, and send them to the table.

Have a chafing-dish on the table, lay some of the slices of venison in the pan of the chafing-dish, throw on a little salt, but not so much as for other meat, a lump of butter, and some currant jelly, put the cover on the dish, let it remain a minute or two, take off the cover, turn the slices of meat, place it on again, and in two or three minutes more the venison will be sufficiently cooked. Each person at the table adds pepper to suit the taste. Some prefer venison cooked without currant jelly.

ROASTED RABBIT.

100. Cut off the head, open and wash it clean, and fill it with a dressing made of bread crumbs, some onions finely chopped, pepper, salt, a little powdered mace, and as much butter as will cause the crumbs to adhere together; sew the rabbit up after the dressing is in, put it on a spit before the fire, and baste it with butter, whilst it is roasting. Or it may be put in a pan with a little water, and baked.

Make a gravy of a gill of water, an ounce of butter, an onion finely chopped, pepper, salt and mace to the taste.

Wine may be added, if preferred.

BAKED RABBIT PIE.

101. Cut a rabbit in pieces, wash it, and season it with salt and pepper. Nearly cover it with cold water, and stew it till it is tender, then add three ounces of butter rolled in flour. If it should not be seasoned sufficiently, add more pepper, as rabbits require more seasoning than many other kinds of meat.

Make a paste, butter your pie dish, and line the sides. Place the pieces of rabbit in the dish, and add just enough of the gravy to keep it from burning, then cover it with a lid of paste, leave an opening on the top, which may be ornamented with strips of paste, and bake it. It should be served in the dish it is baked in. Keep the remainder of the gravy hot, but do not let it boil or simmer, serve it in a gravy boat, or fill the pie with the gravy just before it is sent to the table.

RABBIT POT PIE.

102. Cut a rabbit in small pieces, season it highly with salt and pepper. Make a paste, line the sides of a pot with the crust, then put in the rabbit, with three ounces of butter cut up and rolled in flour. Roll out some of the dough, cut it in pieces about three inches square, and lay it in with the pieces of rabbit; pour in as much water as will cover it, roll out a sheet of paste and place on the top, leaving an opening in the centre. Cover the pot with the lid, and let it cook slowly till the rabbit is done.

If when your pie is nearly done, the gravy should not be thick enough, add a few more pieces of butter rolled in flour.

When the pie is done put the top or soft crust at the bottom of the dish, lay the rabbit on it, then place the brown crust on the top with the brown side up. Serve the gravy in a gravy boat.

FRENCH STEWED RABBIT.

103 Cut a rabbit in pieces, wash it, and put it in a stew-pan with salt, pepper, a little mace, and a quarter of a tea spoonful of ground allspice; put in water enough to keep it from sticking to the pan; cover it closely and let it stew very slowly. When about half done add a quarter of a pound of butter, cut in pieces, and rolled in flour, and half a pint of claret wine. If the meat should not be seasoned enough, add more salt, pepper or spice. Rabbit requires a great deal of seasoning, especially pepper.

Serve it hot. This dish is much esteemed by many Americans.

FRICASEED RABBIT.

104. Cut your rabbit in pieces, wash it and put it in a stew-pan with three gills of water, season it with salt, and *very highly* with pepper, a little mace, and powdered cloves; let it stew very slowly, and when nearly done add three ounces of butter rolled in flour. If you wish a brown fricassee the flour should be browned before it is rolled with the butter; if it is to be a white fricassee, after you stir in the flour and butter add a gill of cream.

SMOTHERED RABBIT.

105. Clean a rabbit, cut off the head, wash it well, and skewer it as if for roasting. Put it in a stew-pan with half a pint of water, some pepper, salt, mace, and cloves, and let it simmer very slowly; keep the stew-pan covered in order to retain the steam. When half done add a quarter of a pound of butter rolled in flour. If the water should stew away too much a little more may be added. Peel some onions and boil them till they are tender, drain and chop them fine, season with salt, pepper and butter to the taste. When the rabbit is done place it upon the dish it is to be served in, then put the onions into the gravy and give them one boil, pour them over the rabbit and serve hot.

ROASTED PIGEONS.

106. Pick the pigeons, draw and wash them; dry them on a clean napkin, rub them inside and outside with pepper and salt; fill them with a dressing of bread crumbs, pepper, salt, butter, and a little onion finely minced; skewer them, or if you choose, tie them round with tape; put them on the spit and baste them frequently with butter. About twenty minutes will cook them.

STEWED PIGEONS.

107. Cut the pigeons down the back, clean them, cut them in four pieces, and wash and wipe

them dry. Put them in a stew-pan, and for each pair of pigeons roll an ounce of butter in a little flour, add some pepper and salt, and water enough just to cover them; stew them till they are tender. If the gravy should not be thick enough add a little more flour.

Pigeons are prepared in the same way for pies.

BROILED SQUAB.

108. Young pigeons or squabs are the nicest for broiling. Cut them down the back, clean them nicely, wash them and dry them on a clean napkin. Have ready a bed of clear coals, heat your gridiron, grease the bars to prevent the pigeons from sticking, and place them over the fire; turn them frequently, and be careful not to let the legs and wings burn. When they are done put them on a dish, season them with pepper and salt, and baste them well with butter on both sides.

PIGEON PIE.

109. This is made in the same manner as chicken pie.

STEWED REED BIRDS, No. 1.

110. Pick the birds, and cut and clean them like chickens. Make a force meat of cold veal, finely chopped with a little grated ham, some pow-

dered nutmeg and mace, and a very small portion of cloves; season the birds inside with pepper and salt, fill them with the dressing, rub them on the outside with pepper and salt, tie the legs down with a piece of thread, which must be cut off when the birds are dished. Place them in the stew-pan with a piece of butter on each and a little flour; put a little water in the bottom of the stew-pan to keep them from burning, and cover them close; when they are tender take them out, cut off the threads, and if the gravy should not be thick enough, add some butter rolled in flour. Pour the gravy over them and serve them hot.

STEWED REED BIRDS, No. 2.

111. Pick and singe them, and with a pair of scissors cut them down the back; or they may be drawn in the same way as chickens. Wash them and dry them on a clean cloth; season with pepper and salt, place a layer of birds at the bottom of your stew-pan, dredge a little flour over them, and add some lumps of butter; then put in another layer of the birds, and so on till all are in. Pour over them just enough water to keep them from burning, cover the stew-pan and let the birds cook slowly. When they are done take them up, and if the gravy is not thick enough, add a little butter rolled in flour, let it boil once and pour it over the birds.

ROASTED REED BIRDS.

112. Pick your birds, and with a pair of scissors cut and draw them as chickens. Wash them clean and wipe them dry; make a dressing of bread crumbs, pepper, salt and butter enough to make the crumbs adhere together; chopped onion may be added, with a small quantity of any kind of sweet herb, finely powdered. Fill the birds with this dressing, sew them up, put them on a spit, and baste them with butter whilst they are roasting.

REED BIRD PIE.

113. Cut your birds in half, wash them and wipe them dry; season with pepper and salt. Line the sides of your pie dish with paste, then place in a layer of reed birds; over these dredge a little flour and put some lumps of butter; then put in another layer of birds, and flour, and butter, till all are in. Put in enough water to make the gravy, cover with a lid of paste, and bake in a moderate oven. Leave an opening in the centre of the top crust to let the steam escape.

FRIED REED BIRDS.

114. Pick them, cut them down the back with a pair of scissors, wash them and dry them in a cloth, season with salt and pepper, dip each one first into some yelk of egg well beaten, then into

bread crumbs or grated cracker, and fry them in hot lard and butter mixed in equal portions.

The white of the egg should not be used, as the bread or cracker crumbs will not adhere to the flesh so well.

They may be dressed as above, and fried in the hot lard and butter, without the egg and crumbs.

ROAST TURKEY.

115. Draw your turkey and prepare it for roasting in the same manner as chickens. Make a dressing of bread crumbs, some onions finely minced, pepper, salt, and a little sweet marjoram, with enough butter to make the crumbs adhere together; rub the inside of the turkey with pepper and salt, fill it with this dressing, season the outside with salt and pepper, truss it firmly, put it on the spit, dredge some flour over it, and place it before the fire; baste it with butter while it is cooking. Clean the giblets, boil them in very little water, with some salt. When the turkey is done take it up, pour the liquor the giblets were boiled in, into the gravy which fell from it, chop up the liver and put it in with some butter rolled in flour to thicken the gravy, and more pepper and salt. Serve it hot, with the gravy in a small tureen. A very good dressing may be made of potatoes boiled and finely mashed with onion, pepper and salt, and

plenty of butter. Some fill the crop with bread and the inside with potatoes.

BOILED TURKEY.

116. Draw your turkey, wash it clean, season it with salt, but no pepper. Make a force-meat of some cold veal finely minced, a little grated ham, pepper and salt to the taste; add also a little grated nutmeg and powdered mace. Fill the crop of the turkey with this force-meat, tie or skewer it well. Dredge flour over it, and wrap it in a napkin. Put it in a large pot with plenty of water which has been salted. Let it boil for about two hours, which will cook it sufficiently, unless it be a very large one.

Take it out of the napkin, place it on a large dish, garnish the edges of the dish with double parsley, and serve with a rich oyster sauce in a tureen.

ROASTED DUCK, No. 1.

117. Clean your ducks nicely, wash them and wipe them dry. Rub them inside with pepper and salt, and fill them with a dressing made of crumbs of bread, two or three onions finely minced, some pepper, salt, and butter enough to make the crumbs adhere. Some use beaten egg in the dressing, but it makes it tough and heavy. After having filled the ducks truss them and put them on the spit; baste them with butter whilst they are roasting.

Wash the livers, first cut out the gall; with a sharp knife open the gizzards by cutting an incision round them, but not so deep as to cut the inner skin; then with your fingers tear them open. Pour boiling water on the feet and skin them; cut off the toes, and crack the leg in half, wash all these. and stew them in very little water, with pepper and salt. When the ducks are done, add the liquor the giblets were boiled in to the gravy, which has dropped from them, and thicken it with a little butter rolled in flour. Serve the liver on the dish with the ducks.

ROAST DUCK, No. 2.

118. Prepare the ducks as directed above, and for the filling, mince two onions finely, add some pepper, salt, and a table spoonful of powdered sage, with an ounce of butter and some beaten egg.

Rub the inside of the ducks with pepper and salt, put in the dressing, truss them, and put them on the spit. For the gravy, proceed as directed above.

ROAST GOOSE.

119. Clean your goose, wash it, and wipe it dry, then season it with pepper and salt both inside and out. Make a dressing of bread crumbs, pepper, salt, butter, a little sweet marjoram, and some onions finely minced. Fill the goose with this dressing, truss it firmly, and put it on the spit.

Whilst it is roasting, baste it with butter, and be careful not to let it burn.

Clean the giblets, put them on in a stew-pan, with very little water, some salt and pepper, and boil them. Add the liquor they were boiled in to the gravy which dripped from the goose. Thicken it with some butter rolled in flour, let it boil a few minutes; add more pepper and salt, if necessary. Pour this gravy in the boat, and serve it with the goose. Some prefer a little sage added to the dressing in place of the sweet marjoram.

A very good dressing for roast goose is to substitute potatoes boiled and finely mashed instead of the bread crumbs, then add the pepper, salt, onions, and sweet marjoram as before.

GIBLET PIE.

120. Wash and clean your giblets, put them in a stew-pan, season with pepper, salt, and a little butter rolled in flour, cover them with water, stew them till they are very tender. Line the sides of your pie dish with paste, put in the giblets, and if the gravy is not quite thick enough add a little more butter rolled in flour. Let it boil once, pour in the gravy, put on the top crust, leaving an opening in the centre of it in the form of a square; ornament this with leaves of the paste. Set the pie in the oven, and when the crust is done take it out.

ROAST CHICKENS.

121. Clean your chickens, wash them and wipe them dry; season them inside with pepper and salt, make a dressing of bread crumbs, some minced onion, pepper, salt, and as much butter as will hold the crumbs together. Fill your chickens with this dressing, skewer them well and season them on the outside with salt and pepper; put them on the spit, dredge a little flour over, and baste them with butter whilst they are roasting.

Boil the gizzards and livers in very little water, take out the liver, chop it up fine, and add it to the water it was boiled in, with a little salt; stir into this all the gravy which dripped from the chickens, and thicken it with some butter rolled in flour.

Partridges are roasted in the same way.

CHICKEN PIE.

122. Cut your chickens in pieces, wash them, and put them in a stew-pan with salt and pepper, and water enough to nearly cover them. To each one, rub one ounce of butter in flour, and add it to the gravy when the chickens are done; let it boil a few minutes. Make a rich paste, line the sides of your pie dish, put in the chickens and half the gravy, cover the pie with the paste; leave an opening in the centre, and ornament the top with paste cut in flowers, or bars twisted and laid across the centre. When the crust is done take out the pie, pour in the remainder of the gravy, and send it to the table in the dish it is baked in. If all the gravy is put in at once it will be apt to boil over the top and disfigure the lid of the pie.

Partridge pies are made in the same manner.

CHICKEN POT PIE.

123. Cut your chickens in pieces, wash them and dry them in a clean napkin; season with salt and pepper. Line the sides of the pot with paste, put in the pieces of chicken, and between every layer of chicken put a piece of butter rolled in flour, with squares of the paste if you choose; pour in enough cold water to cover it, and put on a lid of the paste; leave an opening in the centre of the top crust; cover the pot, place it in front of the fire with a few coals under it. Turn the pot frequently that the crust may be evenly browned all around. When it is done, if the gravy should not be thick enough, add a little more flour mixed with butter. Dish it by putting the top crust on the sides of the dish, lay the chicken in the centre, and place the brown crust on the top. Serve the gravy in a sauce boat.

BROILED CHICKENS.

124. Split them down the back, wash them nicely and wipe them dry. Heat your gridiron, grease the bars, and put your chickens over clear

coals. Broil them nicely, be careful not to burn the legs and wings. When done season them with pepper, salt, and a large piece of butter. Send them to the table hot.

Partridges, pheasants and pigeons are broiled in the same way.

FRIED CHICKENS.

125. Wash your chickens, cut them in pieces, season them with pepper and salt. Have in a pan some hot butter and lard mixed; dust some flour over each piece, and fry them slowly till of a bright brown on both sides; take them up, put a little water in the pan, add some butter rolled in flour to thicken the gravy, and more pepper and salt if required. Young spring chickens are only suitable for frying.

BOILED CHICKENS.

126. Clean and wash your chickens, put them in a pot with boiling water enough to cover them; if the water should boil away add more, as the skin will be discolored if not covered with water. Put enough salt in the water to season the chickens sufficiently when they are done; tie some tape around them to keep them in their proper shape; when they are tender take them up and serve them with rich egg sauce.

Boiled chickens are frequently stuffed with bread

crumbs, seasoned with pepper, salt, a little onion, finely chopped, and some butter; fill the chickens with this dressing, truss them and tie tape around them to preserve their shape. But it is preferable to boil chickens without the filling, as it soaks the water and becomes very insipid.

STEWED CHICKENS.

127. One pair of large chickens,
Two tea spoonsful of salt,
One tea spoonful of pepper,
Eight tea spoonsful of flour,
One pint of water.

Cut up the chickens, separate the thighs from the lower part of the leg, cut the breast in six parts, cut the wings in two parts, and the back in four pieces, put them into a stew-pan with the pepper, salt and flour, stir all well together, and then add the water. Let them stew till perfectly tender. If the gravy should not be thick enough add a little flour mixed with water. Fat chickens require no butter, but early fall chickens would need a quarter of a pound to make a rich gravy.

BROWN FRICASSEE.

128. Cut your chicken in pieces, wash it and wipe it dry; it must be young, an old one would not be tender when cooked in this manner; season it with

pepper and salt. Put in your pan some lard or beef dripping, let it get hot, dredge some flour over your chicken and fry it of a handsome brown, turn each piece so as to have both sides done alike. Take the pieces out, put them on a dish, put a little water in the pan with the gravy, and a piece of butter rolled in brown flour to thicken it. Let it boil once and pour it over the chicken.

WHITE FRICASSEED CHICKEN.

129. Cut up a chicken in pieces, wash it, and season with pepper and salt, put it in a stew-pan with a little water, and let it stew till nearly done; then add a tea cupful of cream and some butter rolled in flour to thicken the gravy. If not sufficiently seasoned, add more pepper or salt as may be required. If the chicken is fat very little butter is necessary. Mace or nutmeg may be added if you like spice.

CHICKEN SALAD, No. 1.

130. A pair of large fowls,

Four table spoonsful of mixed mustard, or eight of French mustard—the French is preferable

Half a pint of vinegar,
Half a pint of sweet oil,
The yelks of ten hard boiled eggs,
One tea spoonful of cayenne pepper,

One tea spoonful of salt,
Six large heads of celery.

Boil the fowls in water which has been salted, and stand them away to cool. Take off the skin, cut the meat in small pieces about a quarter of an inch square, then cut the white part of the celery in very small pieces, put it in a colander, place the colander in a pan of cold water in order to keep the celery crisp.

Boil the eggs till the yelks are hard, which will take twenty minutes; mash the yelks with the oil until they are smooth, then add the vinegar, mustard, pepper and salt.

About fifteen minutes before the chicken salad is to be sent to the table, drain the celery, mix it thoroughly with the chicken, and then pour the dressing over it. Stir it well.

Cold veal or turkey is very good dressed in this way.

This receipt may be relied on as being particularly nice. No. 2 is not quite so rich.

CHICKEN SALAD, No. 2.

131. One pair of chickens,
Eight eggs,
Half a pint of oil,
One gill of vinegar,
Mustard, pepper, and salt to the taste,
Six heads of celery.

Boil the chickens in water with a little salt When cold cut the meat in small pieces about a quarter of an inch square; cut the celery in small pieces and lay it in water; boil the eggs twenty minutes, take out the yelks, mash them fine with the oil, add the vinegar, mustard, salt and pepper. Drain the celery, mix it with the chicken, and stir the mixture of egg, vinegar, oil, &c., well through the chicken and celery.

VEGETABLES.

All vegetables are better to be freshly gathered, when left to stand long, they lose much of their flavor.

Late in the season, when turnips, parsnips, carrots, &c., begin to lose their sweetness, they may be greatly improved by adding a tea spoonful or two of sugar to the water they are boiled in.

BOILED POTATOES, No. 1.

132. Select the potatoes as nearly as possible of the same size. Wash and boil them with the skins on.

Throw a little salt in the water. When they are soft, peel them and send them to the table hot. Or they may be mashed with butter, salt to the taste, and milk or cream in the proportion of an ounce of butter and half a gill of milk or cream to ten potatoes. They should be sent to the table immediately, as they spoil if they stand after they are done.

Put them over the fire, in cold water, or they will be likely to burst before they are cooked.

BOILED POTATOES, No. 2.

133. Wash ten potatoes, boil them in water, with a little salt. When they are soft, peel them, put them in a pan, with an ounce of butter and half a gill of milk or cream. Mash them well, add more salt if necessary, and put them in a vegetable dish.

Have ready an egg beaten light; spread the egg over the potatoes, and brown it with a salamander, if you have one, or wash the pan of the shovel, heat it very hot, and hold it over the potatoes sufficiently near to brown the egg.

Serve it hot.

FRIED POTATOES, No. 1.

134. Boil some potatoes in water a little salted. When they are done, peel them, and set them away to cool. When cold, cut them in thin slices, season with salt and pepper, and dredge a little flour over them.

Have ready some hot lard in a pan, pour in the potatoes, and fry them a delicate brown.

FRIED POTATOES, No. 2.

135. Boil some potatoes; when done, peel them, and set them away to get cold. Then chop them up fine, and add pepper and salt to the taste. Flour them, and fry in hot lard. They must be brown.

Some add a little vinegar just before they are taken out of the pan.

FRIED POTATOES, No. 3.

136. Boil some potatoes, peel, and mash them finely. To ten potatoes add half a gill of milk or cream, and pepper and salt to the taste.

Make the mashed potato in little cakes, flour them on both sides, and fry them in hot lard. If there are any cold mashed potatoes left from dinner, they may be cooked in this way for breakfast.

FRIED POTATOES, No. 4.

137. Boil some potatoes, mash and season them with pepper and salt.

To ten potatoes chop four onions and mix with the mashed potato, and half a gill of milk or cream.

Make it out in small cakes, dredge flour on both sides, and fry them in hot lard till they are of a light brown.

FRIED SWEET POTATOES.

138. Boil some sweet potatoes till they are soft

enough to pass the prong of a fork through them. Peel them, and when they get cold slice them. Season with pepper and salt to the taste, dredge flour over, and fry them in hot lard. They should be of a fine light brown.

ROASTED POTATOES.

139. Wash them, and put them in a pan, in a moderate oven. When they can be easily pierced by a fork, they are done.

Serve them with the skins on. Those who reside in the country, and have wood fires, may roast them in the following manner. Sweep the hot stone in front of the fire, place the potatoes on it, and cover them with hot ashes. When they are soft, wipe the skins and send them to the table hot.

POTATO CAKES.

140. Boil six potatoes, mash them fine, and add to them three eggs, boiled hard and finely chopped, with salt and pepper to the taste, and a table spoonful of milk or cream.

Make it out in small cakes, flour them on both sides, and fry them a delicate brown

POTATO KALE.

141. Six potatoes.
Half head of cabbage.

Two ounces of butter.
One gill of cream.

—

Put your cabbage on to boil, with a little salt in the water; when it is nearly done, pare your potatoes and put them in with the cabbage. When the potatoes are soft, take them out—drain the cabbage—wipe a sauce-pan, or the pot they were boiled in, put the potatoes and cabbage into it, mash both very fine, add the butter and cream with salt and pepper to the taste. Set the pot over the fire and stir it till the potatoes are hot. Serve it immediately.

This is very good with cold meat.

POTATO SALAD.
(*A German Dish.*)

142. Six potatoes.
Six onions.
Two ounces of butter.
Pepper, salt, and vinegar to the taste.

—

Boil the potatoes and the onions till they are soft; the onions require about as long again as the potatoes.

Wipe out the pot in which the potatoes were boiled, mash the onions in it, slice the potatoes, but do not mash them, and add to the onions, put in the butter, pepper, salt, and vinegar; set it over the fire and stir it till it is hot, when it will be ready for the table.

Some persons prefer it without the vinegar.

POTATO SAUSAGE.

143. Of cold veal finely chopped add the same quantity of cold mashed potato, and season with pepper and salt to the taste.

Make it out in small cakes, flour them, and fry them a light brown.

They may be fried in sausage gravy if you have any left.

Cold potatoes left from dinner will answer for this dish.

STEWED TOMATOES.

144. If they are not very ripe, pour boiling water over them, and let them stand a few minutes, the skin will peel off very easily.

Then cut them up, put them in a stew-pan without any water, and cook them till they are soft. If they prove too juicy, dip some of the water out and mash them fine. Season with butter, cayenne pepper and salt.

They may be thickened with bread crumbs or grated cracker, if preferred.

FRIED TOMATOES.

145. Wash them, cut them in half, take out the seeds, and season them with pepper and salt.

Have ready some melted butter in a pan, put them into it, and fry them slowly till very soft.

BAKED TOMATOES.

146. Wash them, and cut them in two parts, round the tomato, that is, so as the cells can be divested of the pulp and seeds which they contain. To six tomatoes take half a pint of bread crumbs, one large onion finely chopped, one ounce of butter, pepper and salt to the taste. Fill the cells of each piece with the dressing, put two halves together, and tie them with a piece of thread. Put them in a pan with an ounce of butter and a gill of water, set them in a moderate oven, and cook them till they are soft.

When done, cut off the threads and serve them.

SCALLOPED TOMATOES.

147. Peel fine ripe tomatoes, cut them up in small pieces, and put in a pan a layer of bread crumbs, then a layer of tomatoes, with pepper, salt and some pieces of butter; then put another layer of bread crumbs and tomatoes, and so on till the dish is full. Spread some beaten egg over the top and set it in the oven and bake it.

BROILED TOMATOES.

148. Wash them, cut them in half, take out the

seeds, grease the bars of your gridiron, put on the tomatoes and broil them slowly. The bars of the gridiron should not be very far apart. When they are done season them with pepper, salt and butter, and serve them hot.

TOMATOES DRESSED AS CUCUMBERS.

149. Peel some tomatoes, cut them in slices, add salt, pepper and vinegar, and serve them cold.

They may be dressed as above with the addition of mustard and sweet oil.

Some prefer them peeled, sliced, and seasoned only with salt.

TOMATO FRICANDEAU.

150. Get some slices of veal cutlets, pound and wash them, season them with pepper and salt, and fry them slowly till they are done. They should be of a light brown on both sides. Stew some tomatoes very dry, strain them through a sieve to get out all the seeds, pour the pulp into the gravy after the meat has been taken out, and thicken it with a piece of butter rolled in flour. Pour this over the meat and serve it hot.

BAKED BEETS.

151. Wash your beets, put them in a pan, and set them in a moderate oven where they will bake

slowly. When they are very soft take them out, remove the skins, slice them, and dress them with butter, pepper and salt, or vinegar if preferred.

They may be boiled and dressed in the same way.

EGG-PLANT, No. 1.

152. Pare and cut them in slices about a quarter of an inch thick, season them with salt and pepper. Have ready some hot butter in a pan, put in the slices and fry them *very slowly* till they are perfectly soft. There should be enough butter in the pan to prevent them from sticking to the bottom. Serve them hot.

EGG-PLANT, No. 2.

153. Make a batter as for fritters. Slice your egg-plant in thin slices not more than the eighth of an inch thick; cut each slice in four parts, or any size you choose, season with pepper and salt, dip each piece in the batter, and fry them in hot lard of a light brown on both sides.

EGG-PLANT, No. 3.

154. Peel your egg-plant and cut it in thin slices, each slice may be cut in four or five pieces according to the size of the plant. Beat some eggs and have ready some bread crumbs or grated

cracker; season your egg-plant, dip each piece in the egg, then in the crumbs, and fry them in hot lard of a handsome brown on both sides.

EGG-PLANT, No. 4.

155. Put on an egg-plant in a vessel of water, and boil it until you can pierce it with a fork, and it is perfectly soft; then take it out, cut it in half, with a spoon scoop out all the inside; season it well with pepper and salt, have some bread crumbs or grated cracker and beaten egg. Take up a portion of the egg-plant about the size of an oyster, with a spoon, dip it into the egg, then into the crumbs, and fry them in hot lard of a light brown on both sides.

EGG-PLANT, No. 5.
(*French mode.*)

156. Cut an egg-plant in half, but do not cut off the rind. Then with a sharp knife score it very deeply, both lengthwise and crosswise, but be careful not to break the skin in so doing. Place each half in a pan with the scored side up, season it with pepper and salt, and over this pour some sweet oil or melted butter, if preferred. Set it in an oven and cook it slowly till the plant is perfectly soft. The top should be brown.

BROWNED EGG-PLANT.

157. Boil an egg-plant in water which has been salted, until it is perfectly soft; when done take it out of the water, cut it in half and scoop out all the inside, mash it very fine, and to every tea cupful of mashed egg-plant add one table spoonful of grated cracker and a dessert spoonful of butter, with salt and pepper to the taste. Put it in the dish it is to be served in, beat an egg light, spread a portion of it over the egg-plant, then strew on some grated cracker, and lastly spread over the remainder of the egg. Set it in the oven and brown it. Serve it hot.

PARSNIPS, No. 1.

158. Scrape and wash your parsnips and put them on with just enough water to boil them and no more; when they are done they should be nearly dry. Then dish them and pour over melted butter and a little salt, or some drawn butter.

PARSNIPS, No. 2.

159. Boil them as directed in No. 1, and when done cut them in half, grease the bars of your gridiron, put them on it over some lively coals and brown them.

PARSNIPS, No. 3.

160. Boil them as directed in No. 1, when

done mash them, season with pepper and salt, and a small piece of butter.

PARSNIPS, No. 4.

161. Boil them as in No. 1, slice, flour and fry them of a light brown in some hot lard.

PARSNIPS STEWED.

162. Put on a piece of pickled pork and boil until it is about half done or a little more. Then scrape and wash your parsnips, put them on in as little water as will keep them from burning, then add the pork; when the parsnips are soft dish them.

BOILED GREEN CORN.

163. Green corn should always be boiled on the cob, with the inner husks on it. To prepare it turn down the inner husks, cut off the upper end, wash the corn, and replace the husks.

Boil it about half an hour in water salted to the taste. It should be cooked in just enough water to cover it.

CORN FRITTERS.

164. One tea cupful of milk.
Three eggs.
One pint of green corn grated.

A little salt.

As much flour as will form a batter.

———

Beat the eggs, the yelks and whites separate. To the yelks of the eggs add the corn, salt, milk, and flour enough to form a batter, beat the whole very hard, then stir in the whites, and drop the batter, a spoonful at a time, into hot lard, and fry them on both sides of a light brown color.

CORN OYSTERS.

165. One pint of grated green corn.

Two eggs.

As much wheat flour as will make it adhere together.

———

Beat the eggs, mix them with the grated corn, and add enough flour to form the whole into a paste. Fry them of a light brown in hot lard.

HOMINY.

166. One quart of hominy or broken corn to one pint of beans; pick and wash them, and put them to soak with water enough just to cover them. Let them soak all night; in the morning put all on to boil, with three pounds of pickled pork, and more water to cover them. Boil it eight hours. The pot will require filling up with hot water, whilst the hominy is boiling. It requires no stirring.

SOUR KROUT

167. Six heads of cabbage.
Half a gill of salt.

Wash the cabbages nicely, line the tub with the outer leaves, and sprinkle over a little of the salt. Cut the cabbages very fine, and put in a layer of cabbage and a sprinkle of salt until the whole is in. Each layer of cabbage must be well pounded down with a heavy pestle. Cover the top with cabbage leaves and a little more salt. Spread over the whole a clean cloth, and then a board to fit closely, with a weight to press the cabbage down.

As soon as fermentation ceases, take off the board and cloth, wash them well, and replace them. The sour krout will now be fit for use.

BOILED SOUR KROUT.

168. One quart of sour krout.
One pound of pickled pork.

Put on the sour krout to boil, wash the pork and put with it; at the end of two hours take out the pork, but let the krout boil one hour longer.

CAULIFLOWER.

169. Wash a fine cauliflower, put it in a net and boil it in just enough water to cover it. The water must be salted to the taste.

When it is done drain it, put it in a vegetable dish, and pour drawn butter over it.

COLD SLAW.

170. Cut a cabbage in half, and with a sharp knife shave it down very finely.

Make a dressing of one egg, well beaten, half a gill of vinegar, salt to taste, and a tea spoonful of butter. Beat the egg light, add to it the vinegar, salt, and butter. As soon as the egg is thick, take it off the fire, set it away to cool, then pour it over the cabbage, and mix it well together.

Some prefer a little sugar in the egg and vinegar.

HOT SLAW.

171. Cut the cabbage in half, and shave it very finely. Put it into a stew-pan, with a piece of butter, and salt to the taste; pour in just enough water to prevent it from sticking to the pan. Cover it closely, and let it stew, stir it frequently, and when it is quite tender, add a little vinegar, and serve it hot.

FRENCH SLAW.

172. Shave the cabbage as for other slaw.

To one pint of the cut cabbage, have three eggs boiled hard, mash the yelks with a spoon, and add gradually one wine glassful of oil, then pour in one wine glass of vinegar, one tea spoonful of common mustard, or a dessert spoonful of French mustard, salt and cayenne pepper to the taste.

Pour the mixture over the cabbage, stir it well, and serve it.

MUSHROOMS.

173. Wash your mushrooms, cut off the end of the stalks, and peel them. Put them in a stewpan, without any water, and season with salt and pepper. Add two ounces of butter rolled in two tea spoonsful of flour, to every pint of mushrooms. Cover them closely, and let them simmer slowly till they are soft.

SPINACH.

174. Wash it well through several waters, as it is apt to be gritty. Put it into a pot without any water, let it cook slowly until it is very soft. Then drain and mash it with a piece of butter, pepper and salt to the taste. Put it in a vegetable dish, and strew over the top eggs which have been boiled hard and finely chopped, or poached eggs.

SPINACH AS GREENS.

175. Spinach may be boiled with a piece of corned beef, or pickled pork, and served as greens.

Cabbage may be boiled in the same manner, but meat has a very strong taste when boiled with vegetables in this way.

DANDELION.

176. Pick and wash your dandelion and cut off the roots. Drain it, and make a dressing of an egg, well beaten, a half a gill of vinegar, a tea spoonful of butter, and salt to the taste. Mix the egg, vinegar, butter and salt together, put the mixture over the fire, and as soon as it is thick, take it off, and stand it away to get cold.

Drain your dandelion, pour the dressing over it and send it to the table.

SQUASHES OR CYMLINS.

177. If they are old and tough peel them, but if they are young, and the rind is tender, they are better cooked with the skin on.

The round squashes may be cooked whole, but the long ones must be cut in two or three pieces, according to the size of the vessel they are to be cooked in.

Stew them in as little water as possible, till they are soft. Take them out, drain, and press them as dry as you can. Then put them in a stew-pan, add butter, pepper and salt to the taste. Add some cream if you have it.

Heat them very hot and serve them.

OCHRAS.

178. Wash them, cut them in half, season with

pepper and salt; fry them in butter till of a light brown. They must be fried slowly.

CARROTS.

179. Scrape and wash them. Boil them in a little water, with salt to taste. When they are soft dish them, and pour over melted butter, or drawn butter.

TURNIPS.

180. They should be boiled in as little water as possible. Season the water with salt just to taste. When they begin to lose their sweetness, late in the season, add a little sugar, which greatly improves their flavor.

When soft, take them up and mash them with a little pepper, salt, butter, and cream, if you have it.

CELERY DRESSED AS SLAW.

181. Cut the celery in pieces about a quarter of an inch long. Make a dressing of the yelks of three eggs boiled hard, half a gill of vinegar, half a gill of sweet oil, one tea spoonful of French mustard, or half a tea spoonful of common mustard, with salt and cayenne pepper to the taste. Pour this mixture over the celery, stir it well and send it to the table.

It should be kept in cold water to make it crisp,

until about fifteen minutes before it is sent to the table, then drain it and pour the dressing over.

CELERY STEWED WITH LAMB.
(French fashion.)

182. Take six neck chops, crack the bone of each across the middle, and put them into a stew-pan. Cut up and wash two large heads of celery, and mix with the meat; pepper and salt to the taste. Roll two ounces of butter in a little flour and add to it, with half a gill of water. Cover it closely, and let it simmer slowly till the celery is soft. If the gravy stews away too much, add a little water, and if it should not be quite thick enough, stir in a little flour mixed with cold water.

ASPARAGUS.

183. Scrape and wash your asparagus, put it in a net, boil it in just enough water to cover it, with salt to the taste.

When it is done and perfectly soft, take it up, drain it, and pour over it a rich drawn butter.

Toast is generally laid in the bottom of the dish and the asparagus put on it, but some prefer it without the toast.

DUTCH SALAD.

184. Choose a head of fine cabbage lettuce,

strip off the outer leaves, cut it in half, and wash it well.

Fry a slice of ham; when it is done, take it out of the pan, and pour in to the hot fat one beaten egg, and a wine glassful of vinegar, set it on the fire, and as soon as it thickens take it off.

Cut the salad in small pieces, and pour the egg and vinegar over it whilst it is lukewarm.

Lay the salad in a deep dish, cut the ham in pieces about an inch square, and place on the top. Let it stand about five minutes, and send it to the table.

CORN SALAD.

185. This may be dressed at the table with sugar and vinegar, or lemon juice; or with eggs boiled hard, vinegar, mustard, sweet oil, salt and pepper as directed for French slaw.

Scurvy grass and lettuce may be dressed in the same manner.

BOILED ONIONS.

186. Peel them, and boil them in equal parts of milk and water. When they are tender, take them up, drain them, and add salt, pepper and butter to the taste.

Do not put salt in the water they are boiled in, as that will curdle the milk and cause a scum to settle on the onions.

FRIED CUCUMBERS.

187. Slice your cucumbers lengthwise, season them with pepper and salt, flour and fry them in hot butter. They should be of a delicate brown color when done.

LIMA BEANS.

188. Lima beans require from half an hour to three quarters to boil. They should be boiled in as little water as possible to preserve their flavor. As soon as they are soft take them out, drain them in a colander and season with butter, pepper and salt; pour them in a pan to be seasoned, as the butter would run through the colander.

Add salt to the water they are boiled in.

WINDSOR OR HORSE BEANS.

189. Shell the beans, put them in a pan, and pour boiling water over them, cover them and let them stand where they will keep warm. In fifteen minutes pour off the water and remove the thick brown skin which gives them such a strong flavor when boiled with it on. Put them in a stew-pan with very little water, and boil them till they are soft. Drain them and season with butter, pepper and salt.

STRINGED BEANS.

190. Prepare the beans by cutting each end and

stripping off the tough fibre, commonly known as the string; cut each bean in three or four pieces, and stew them in very little water, which has been salted, so that when they are done the pan will be nearly dry. They require from one to two hours to boil. When they are perfectly soft drain them in a colander, then put them in a pan and season with butter, pepper and salt to the taste. Serve them hot.

BOILED DRIED BEANS.

191. Put a piece of pickled pork in a pot with two quarts of water. In another pot put one quart of dried beans, which must have been carefully picked and washed. As soon as the beans begin to boil take them out, put them in a colander to drain, then put them in with the meat and just cover the whole with water. Boil them till they are quite soft and send them to the table.

GREEN PEAS.

192. These should be boiled in very little water, with a tea spoonful of salt to a pint of water, and if the peas are not very sweet add a little sugar. When they are young fifteen minutes is sufficient to boil them. Drain them and add butter, pepper and salt to the taste.

SALSIFY OR OYSTER-PLANT, No. 1.

193. Scrape the roots, wash and boil them in water with a little salt. When they are soft take them up, drain them and season to the taste with pepper, and more salt if necessary. For ten roots pour over half an ounce of melted butter.

SALSIFY OR OYSTER-PLANT, No. 2.

194. Boil the roots in water, with a little salt, until they are soft. Take them up, mash them very fine, add pepper and salt to the taste. Have ready some bread crumbs or grated cracker, and a couple of eggs beaten. With a spoon dip out a portion of the salsify about as large as an oyster, dip it in the egg, then in the cracker, and fry it in hot lard. When of a light brown on both sides lay them on a dish and send to the table. This is a breakfast dish.

SALSIFY OR OYSTER-PLANT, No. 3.

195. Wash the roots and scrape them clean; grate them and add a little pepper and salt; beat two eggs, add a pint of milk, and stir in enough flour to make a thick batter, also salt to the taste. Mix the salsify with the batter, and have ready a pan with some hot lard, dip out a spoonful of the batter and drop in the pan, then another close by the first, and so on. Turn the fritters, and when

they are of a light brown on both sides they are done.

They resemble oyster fritters.

SALSIFY OR OYSTER-PLANT, No. 4.

196. Boil the roots till tender, mash them and season with salt to the taste. Make a batter as directed in No. 3, mix the salsify with it, and proceed as before.

SAUCES.

APPLE SAUCE.

197. Pare, core and slice your apples, put them in a kettle with water enough to keep them from burning, cover them, and as soon as they are soft mash them very fine. When they are nearly cold sweeten them to the taste.

Quince sauce is made in the same manner.

LEMON SAUCE.

198. Half a pint of water,
    Five ounces of nice *brown* sugar,
    Two ounces of butter,
    Three tea spoonsful of flour,
    The rind of a lemon grated, and some of the juice.

Mix the flour smoothly with a little cold water,

and stir it into half a pint of boiling water, let it boil one minute, then add the sugar, the butter, and the grated rind of one lemon. Stir in as much of the lemon juice as will make it an agreeable acid. Some prefer nutmeg and vinegar to the lemon.

To be served hot.

YORKSHIRE SAUCE.

199. Three ounces of butter,
Five table spoonsful of powdered sugar,
Three drops of essence of lemon,
Nutmeg or cinnamon to the taste

Beat the butter and sugar to a cream, and add the lemon and spice.

This sauce is eaten with baked puddings, **fritters,** &c. Some add a tea spoonful of brandy.

NUN'S BUTTER.

200. Take equal portions of butter and sugar; beat them well together, then add cinnamon and nutmeg to the taste.

DRIED PEACH SAUCE.

201. Pick your fruit, wash it through several waters; then pour as much hot water on as will cover it, and let it stand all night. The next morning put the fruit, and the water it was soaked in,

into a preserving kettle, and stew the peaches till they are very soft; when done pass the fruit through a colander to make it perfectly smooth, sweeten it to your taste, put it back in the stew-pan and let it boil once. Stand it away to cool.

CRANBERRY SAUCE.

202. Pick and wash your cranberries, and add half a tea-cup of water to a quart; stew them till they will mash, then add the sugar; let them boil a few minutes, and pour them while warm into the dishes they are to be served in.

WINE SAUCE.

203. Two gills of water,
   Two table spoonsful of brown sugar,
   Two small tea spoonsful of flour,
   One ounce of butter,
   One gill of wine.

Stir the sugar into the water, and as soon as it boils add the flour, which should be mixed smoothly with a little cold water. Let it boil one minute, then take it off the fire, and add the butter and wine. It should be sent to the table warm. Add ground cinnamon to your taste.

RICH WINE SAUCE.

204. Half a pint of boiling water,

Five ounces of sugar,
Three ounces of butter,
Two gills of wine.

Mix the flour to a smooth paste with a little cold water, stir this into the half pint of boiling water. Let it boil about one minute. Take it off, and add the sugar, (brown is the best,) butter, and wine. Some prefer a little nutmeg.

Serve it hot.

CREAM SAUCE.

205. Boil a pint of cream, sweetened very well with white sugar, and flavored with grated lemon-peel, or vanilla.

Let it boil once, then take it off the fire and strain it.

Serve it hot or cold, according to the dishes it is to be eaten with.

VEGETABLE SAUCE.

206. Take equal quantities of ripe tomatoes and young ochras; chop the ochras fine, skin the tomatoes, and slice an onion. Put all into a stew-pan, with half an ounce of butter, salt and pepper to the taste. Stew it very slowly. When the vegetables are tender serve it.

With cold meat this sauce is very good.

TOMATO MUSTARD.

207. Cut a peck of tomatoes in small pieces, boil them till tender. Rub them through a sieve to extract the pulp, which put on and boil until nearly dry. Then add one table spoonful of cayenne pepper, one table spoonful of black pepper, one tea spoonful of cloves, two table spoonsful of mustard seed, and two table spoonsful of salt. Boil the whole a few moments, and when cold bottle it and cork it tightly.

If this should not be quite salt enough, a little more may be added before it is boiled the last time.

Put a table spoonful of sweet oil on the top of each bottle before it is corked, to exclude the air.

EGG SAUCE.

208. Boil half a pint of milk, and stir into it as much flour mixed with cold water as will thicken it. Then take it off the fire, and beat in gradually three ounces of butter; add a little salt. Boil two eggs hard; chop them finely, and add them to the milk and butter.

This sauce is used for boiled chicken or fish.

DRAWN BUTTER.

209. Boil half a pint of milk, and stir into it as much wheat flour mixed with cold milk, as will thicken it. Take it off the fire and beat in gradually three ounces of butter. Add a little salt.

This is poured over asparagus and some other vegetables.

ONION SAUCE.

210. Peel the onions, put them on to boil in equal portions of milk and water, but no salt, as it will curdle the milk. When soft, drain them in a colander, put them in a pan, chop them up finely, and add butter, pepper and salt to the taste. Onions for sauce ought to be white.

MINT SAUCE.

211. Choose some young mint, pick and wash it; chop it very fine, and pour on enough vinegar to wet it. To every gill of vinegar allow two gills of brown sugar.

The sugar should be dissolved in the vinegar, then poured on the mint.

MUSHROOM SAUCE.

212. Peel and wash a quart of mushrooms, put them in a stew-pan, with a little salt, pepper, and two ounces of butter. Cover the stew-pan, and simmer them slowly till they are tender. Mix smoothly one tea spoonful of flour with a gill of cream, stir this into the mushrooms, let them boil once, and serve them.

Mace, nutmeg, and cloves may be stewed with this sauce, if spices are preferred.

PARSLEY SAUCE.

213. Make some drawn butter, (see No. 209,) and whilst it is warm stir into it some parsley finely chopped.

CAPER SAUCE.

214. Make a half-pint of drawn butter, (see No. 209,) and into this stir half a wine-glass of capers with two table spoonsful of vinegar.

HASLET SAUCE.
(For roast Pig.)

215. Put on the feet and liver of the pig with just enough water to cover them, with a little salt. Let them stew slowly, when the feet are tender take them up, cut them in two or three pieces, but do not take out the bones; chop the liver, return it and the feet to the liquor they were boiled in; set the stew-pan over the fire, add pepper, salt and sweet-marjoram to the taste. Roll a piece of butter in flour, and stir in to thicken the gravy, add two glasses of port wine and serve it hot.

Any kind of spice may be added.

HORSE RADISH SAUCE.

216. Grate a stick of horse-radish, mix with it as much vinegar as will cover it, and a tea spoonful of sugar, with a little salt.

This is generally eaten with roast beef or cold meat.

FRENCH TOMATO SAUCE.

217. Peel your tomatoes and cut them in small pieces. Make a dressing for six tomatoes of a table spoonful of sweet oil, one table spoonful of vinegar, half a tea spoonful of common mustard, or one tea spoonful of French mustard, cayenne pepper and salt to the taste. Pour this dressing over the tomatoes, stir them well and serve them.

Tomatoes may be dressed as cucumbers, and make a very good sauce for cold meat.

OYSTER SAUCE.

218. Cut off the beards and boil them with the liquor with a bit of mace and lemon peel. In the mean time throw the oysters in cold water and then drain them; strain the spice from the liquor, put it into a sauce-pan with the oysters, with two ounces of butter rolled in flour, and a gill of rich milk or cream. Let it boil once, squeeze in a little lemon juice, and serve it hot.

TOMATO SAUCE.

219. Wash a dozen tomatoes, cut them in pieces but do not skin them. Put them in a stew-pan with salt, cayenne pepper, one tea spoonful of whole allspice, half a dozen cloves, and four or five blades of mace. Stew them slowly till they are soft, pass them through a sieve to remove the skins and spice; put them back in the stew-pan, let them

boil five minutes, then add two ounces of butter rolled in half a tea spoonful of flour, let it boil once, then serve it.

PICKLES.

Pickles should always be done in the very best cider or wine vinegar, as the chemical preparations known by the name of vinegar soften the pickles, besides being very injurious to the stomach.

Stone or glass jars are the best for keeping pickles, which should be always completely covered with vinegar. When they are first put into the jars they require attention for a day or two, to keep them filled up, as the vinegar sinks in the jar, or is imbibed by the pickles.

PICKLED PEPPERS.

220. If you would prefer your peppers less pungent, cut an opening in the top of the pepper, and take out half the seeds.

Lay them for two weeks in salt and water which will bear an egg. Be careful to keep them covered with the brine. Put a board over them to keep them under the salt and water, and take off the scum as it rises.

If they are not yellow at the end of two weeks, let them remain in the brine a little longer.

When yellow take them out, wash them, and put

them in a kettle with cold water—cover the top with leaves—place them near the fire, let them get hot, but do not permit them to simmer. When they are greened in this manner, take them out, drain them, place them in your jars, and pour cold spiced vinegar over them.

If you wish to stuff them, chop some cabbage very fine, season it highly with mace, cinnamon, cloves, and mustard seed—stuff the peppers with this preparation, and tie a thread round each one to keep the stuffing in.

PICKLED MUSHROOMS, No. 1.

221. Choose button mushrooms; wipe them well with a clean cloth. Sprinkle a little salt over them, and put them in a stew-pan, with some pieces of mace and whole pepper corns. Simmer them slowly till all the juice is out of them. Shake them frequently. Let them simmer very gradually till all the liquor is dried up, but be careful not to let the mushrooms get dry. When the juice has all evaporated, pour over them as much cold vinegar as will cover them, let them get hot, and put them in jars. When cold, cover them closely.

PICKLED MUSHROOMS, No. 2.

222. Select the *button* mushrooms, that is, those which are not fully blown. Cut off the ends of

the stems, scrape them, peel the tops, and wipe them on a clean cloth.

Put them into a stew-pan, with just enough water to prevent them from sticking to the bottom of the pan. Shake them occasionally, to prevent them from burning.

As soon as they are tender, pour over them some boiling vinegar, seasoned with mace, cloves, whole grains of pepper, and salt.

When cool, bottle them, and seal the corks.

PICKLED ONIONS.

223. Choose small white onions, peel them, and throw a few at a time in a pan of boiling salt and water; as soon as they look clear take them out carefully, and place them on a sieve to dry; then put in more, and so on, till all are cooked. When they are cold, put them in jars, and pour spiced vinegar over them.

To each quart of the vinegar, put one table spoonful of whole allspice, half a table spoonful of pepper grains, three or four small pieces of mace, half a dozen cloves, and a table spoonful of mustard seed. Boil all these spices in the vinegar, and pour it, boiling hot, over the pickles.

PICKLED EGGS.

224. Boil some eggs hard; take off the shells,

put them into a jar, and cover them with cold vinegar.

CHOW CHOW.

225. Three cabbages,
Twenty-five peppers,
Half a pint of mustard seed,
Three sticks of horse-radish, chipped.

Cut the cabbages as for slaw; chop the peppers very fine. Put in a jar a layer of cabbage, a very little salt, then a layer of peppers, sprinkle over this some horse-radish and mustard seed, and so on, till all is in, then fill up the jars with cold vinegar, in every quart of which dissolve two ounces of sugar.

This is very good with hot or cold meat.

PICKLED WALNUTS.

226. Rub your walnuts well with a coarse towel, and lay them for two weeks in salt and water strong enough to float an egg.

Drain them, and put them in your kettle, with fresh water enough to cover them, and let them stand twelve hours, where they will keep hot, but not boil.

To one hundred walnuts take one gallon of the best vinegar, one ounce of pepper, one ounce of cloves, half an ounce of mace, half an ounce of nutmeg, four ounces of ginger. Break the ginger and nutmegs in pieces, bruise the pepper a little, and put the spices into the vinegar just before it boils. Let it boil five minutes; pour it out, cover it closely, and stand it away to get cold.

Place the walnuts in your jars, and strew over them about four ounces of mustard seed, pounded and sifted, then pour the spiced vinegar over and cover them closely.

PICKLED PEACHES.

227. Select ripe cling-stone peaches. To one gallon of good vinegar add four pounds of brown sugar; boil this for a few minutes, and take off any scum which may rise. Rub the peaches with a flannel cloth, to remove the down, and stick a clove in each; put them in glass or stone jars, and pour the liquor upon them boiling hot. When cold, cover the jars and let them stand in a cool place for a week or ten days, then pour off the liquor and boil it as before, after which return it, boiling, to the peaches, which should be carefully covered and stored away for future use.

If your peaches are very hard, boil them in water till tender, before you pickle them, and they will be fit for use almost immediately.

PICKLED BEANS.

228. String-beans, or French beans, are the

10*

kind used for pickling. Take off the strings but do not break the beans; put them in strong salt and water for three or four days; cover them with a board and weight so as to keep them under the water. Then take them out, wash them, and put them in a preserving kettle with hot water enough to cover them, and put leaves or a cloth over them to keep in the steam. When they are green take them out, drain them and put them in jars; pour hot vinegar over them, with any kind of spice you may like best, and a small piece of alum in each jar.

Radish pods are pickled in the same way.

PICKLED MANGOES.

229. Cut your mangoes in half, take out all the seeds, tie them together with coarse thread, and lay them in strong salt and water for three or four days. Then wash and drain them, put them into a kettle with vine or cabbage leaves over the top, or they may be covered with a clean coarse cloth; pour in hot water enough to cover them, and let them stand near the fire to keep hot. When they are green take them out, untie them, turn the cut side down and drain them. Cut some horse-radish in fine slips, and mix with it some mace, cloves, pepper, allspice and mustard seed; fill your mangoes with this, and if you like it add a clove of garlic to each one, place the two sides together and tie them again. Put them in jars and cover them

with vinegar. Cut off the threads before they are sent to the table.

PICKLED CUCUMBERS.

230. Select the small sized cucumbers for pickling. They should be free from bruises and of a fine green color, for if they are old and yellow when picked from the vines they will never be green when they are pickled. Wash your cucumbers in cold water to remove all the sand and grit, put them in your pickling tub, make a brine of salt and water strong enough to float an egg. Pour enough of this brine over the cucumbers to cover them; spread over the top a coarse cloth and over this put the lid of the tub, which should be just large enough to fit inside and slip down so as to press on the cucumbers, put a weight on the lid to keep it in its place. Let them stand in the salt and water till they are perfectly yellow, which will be in about nine days. When they are quite yellow take them out, wash them in cold water and examine each one separately; if you should find any soft or bruised reject them, as they would be likely to spoil the others. Put them into a preserving kettle, cover them with hot water and vine or cabbage leaves, or if you have no leaves a clean coarse towel will answer as well. Put a plate over the top and stand them where they will keep hot, but not simmer, as that would ruin them. When they

are perfectly green take them out of the water, drain them, and put in your jars first a layer of cucumbers, then a tea spoonful of whole allspice, half a dozen cloves, some strips of horse-radish, and half a tea spoonful of mustard seed, then more cucumbers, and so on till the jar is full. Pour in as much good vinegar as will cover them, with a tea spoonful of pulverized alum to each jar. In a day or two examine them, and fill up the jars with vinegar if the pickles have absorbed it so as to leave the top ones uncovered.

If you do not wish to pickle all your cucumbers at once, (and they are much better when they are freshly pickled,) take them out of the salt and water, wash and drain them. Put the brine over the fire, boil and skim it; let it stand to get cold; wash the pickle tub, wipe it dry, put the cucumbers into it; examine each one that no specked ones may be put in the tub, pour the cold brine over them, wash the cloth and lid of the tub and replace them as before. Cucumbers will keep in this way all winter. They may be pickled a few at a time whenever they are wanted. They must be soaked twenty-four hours in cold water before they are pickled; if they are so long in salt and water they imbibe too much salt to green them without soaking.

Gherkins are done in the same way.

PICKLED BEETS.

231. Boil your beets till tender, but not quite soft. To four large beets boil three eggs hard, remove the shells; when the beets are done take off the skin by laying them for a few minutes in cold water and then stripping it off; slice them a quarter of an inch thick, put the eggs at the bottom, and then put in the beets with a little salt. Pour on cold vinegar enough to cover them. The eggs imbibe the color of the beets, and look beautiful on the table.

PICKLED CHERRIES.

232. Pick over your cherries, remove all the specked ones. Put them into a jar, and pour over them as much hot vinegar and sugar as will cover them; to each gallon of vinegar allow four pounds of sugar. Boil and skim it and pour it hot over the fruit. Let it stand a week, then pour off the vinegar and boil it as before, pour it hot over the cherries the second time. As soon as they are cold tie them closely.

TOMATO CATSUP, No. 1.

233. Boil half a bushel of tomatoes until they are soft, squeeze them through a fine wire sieve and add—

One quart of vinegar,

Half a pint of salt,
One ounce of cloves,
Two ounces of *whole* allspice,
Two ounces of ground cayenne pepper,
A dessert spoonful of ground black pepper,
Two heads of garlic skinned and separated.

—

Mix the whole together and boil three hours; bottle without straining it.

On the top of each bottle pour a table spoonful of sweet oil, cork them closely and seal them. The sweet oil by excluding the air tends to preserve the catsup.

—

TOMATO CATSUP, No. 2.

234. Slice the tomatoes, put a layer in a deep vessel, and sprinkle over some salt; then another layer of tomatoes and salt till all are in. Stand them in the sun for two or three days, when they are soft pass them through a sieve, and put the pulp, thus drained out, over the fire to boil. Add cayenne pepper, whole black pepper, mace, cloves, allspice, and a little race ginger if you like; let it boil till it is thick, add a clove of garlic; by tasting it you can judge if it is seasoned to your taste. When cold, bottle it off; put a table spoonful of sweet oil on the top of each bottle, and seal the corks.

MUSHROOM CATSUP.

235. Procure fresh mushrooms, pick them carefully, wipe them clean, and put a layer in the bottom of a pan, sprinkle over some salt, then another layer of mushrooms and more salt until all are in; cover the pan and let them stand two days, mash them well and strain them through a hair sieve. To each quart of the pulp add one ounce and a half of whole black pepper, half an ounce of whole allspice, and a few blades of mace. Boil it till reduced to two-thirds the original quantity. When done pour it in a pan and stand it away till the next day, then pass it through a hair sieve and bottle it for use. Put it in small bottles, on the top of each pour a table spoonful of sweet oil to exclude the air. Cork them closely and rosin the corks.

WALNUT CATSUP.

236. When your pickled walnuts are soft, mash them through the vinegar which covers them, strain it and boil it to a proper thickness. Bottle it, put a table spoonful of sweet oil on the top of each bottle, and cork them tightly; seal the corks and it will keep for several years.

This catsup is excellent.

PICKLED NASTURTIUMS.

237. Cut the green seeds of the nasturtiums

with a piece of the stem to each. Put them in a jar of cold vinegar.

PICKLED TOMATOES.

238. Take one peck of ripe tomatoes, prick them with a large needle, and lay them in strong salt and water eight days. Then take them out of the brine and lay them in vinegar and water for twenty-four hours. Scald a dozen small onions in vinegar and stand the whole away to get cold. Drain the tomatoes and add them to the cold onions and vinegar, with two wine-glasses of mustard-seed and an ounce of cloves.

PASTRY.

The flour for pastry should be of the whitest and finest quality. It should be mixed with a broad knife, as the moisture and warmth of the hand makes it heavy.

The butter should be of the best quality, as if it is a little rancid it will taste. To make puff paste it should have all the salt washed out of it.

Iron, or block tin plates are the best for baking pastry.

Always use cold water (in summer iced water) to mix pastry, and if it cannot be baked immediately, set it away in a cool place.

PUFF-PASTE.

239.   One pound of butter,
   One pound of flour.

Wash your butter in cold water to extract al. the salt; work it well with a broad wooden spoon in order to get out all the water. Lay it between clean napkins, put it in a tin pan or plate, set it on the ice to get hard, but do not let it freeze. Sift your flour in a pan, cut the butter in four equal parts, cut one-fourth in very small pieces in the flour, but do not touch it, as the warmth of your hands will make the paste heavy. Add to the flour as much *cold* water as will make it a stiff dough. Turn it out on your pie-board, roll it gently into sheets, cut one-third of the remainder of the butter into small pieces, and lay over it, sprinkle on a **very** little flour, fold it over, roll it out again, cut one-half of the butter which is left in small pieces and lay on, put on a little flour, and fold it as before, roll it out again, and put on the remainder of the butter. It should now be set on the ice, but should not come in contact with it. When it is perfectly cold, roll it out in a sheet thinner in the centre than at the edges of your pie, cut it with a *very sharp* knife the size you wish it. Fill with whatever you choose, and bake in a tolerably quick oven.

PLAIN PASTE.

240. One pound of flour,
Three-quarters of butter.

Put the ingredients together in the same manner as directed for puff paste.

COMMON PASTE.

241. One pound of flour,
Half a pound of butter.

Proceed as directed for puff-paste, only the butter need not be washed, nor the paste placed upon the ice.

A very good paste may be made with the above quantity of flour, and a quarter of a pound of butter, and the same quantity of nice fresh lard.

LEMON PUDDING, No. 1.

242. Half a pound of sugar,
Half a pound of butter,
Five eggs,
The grated rind and juice of one lemon,
Half a gill of brandy.

Beat the butter and sugar. Whisk the eggs and add to it the grated *yellow* rind and juice of one lemon, and lastly the liquor. Make a puff-paste,

line your pie plates with it, and pour in the mixture. These ingredients will make three puddings.
It requires a moderate oven.

This is a very rich and expensive kind of pudding—for a plainer kind see No. 2.

In place of the liquor, a table spoonful of rose water, and a tea spoonful of grated nutmeg may be added.

LEMON PUDDING, No. 2.

243. Half a pound of sugar,
A quarter of a pound of butter,
Five eggs,
The grated yellow rind and juice of one lemon.

Beat the butter and sugar to a cream. Whisk the eggs and add to it, then stir in the lemon juice and grated rind.

Make a paste, cover your pie plates, pour in the mixture, and bake in a moderate oven.

Two table spoonsful of brandy may be added, if preferred, to flavor it.

ORANGE CHEESE-CAKE.

244. A quarter of a pound of butter,
A quarter of a pound of sugar,
Three eggs,
A wine glass of milk or cream,
Two ounces of sponge cake,

The rind of one orange grated,
Half a nutmeg,
One table spoonful of brandy, or two of rose water.

Pour the milk or cream over the sponge cake to moisten it. Then stir together your butter and sugar, whisk your eggs, mash the cake very fine, and mix all together with the liquor and spice.

Line your pie plates with paste, fill with the mixture, and bake in a moderate oven.

LEMON CHEESE-CAKE.

245. A quarter of a pound of butter,
A quarter of a pound of sugar,
A wine glass of milk or cream,
Two ounces of sponge cake,
Three eggs,
The grated rind of one and juice of half a lemon.

Slice the cake, and pour over it the milk or cream. Beat the butter and sugar together, and stir into it. Mash the sponge cake very fine, and add to the above. Grate the yellow rind, and squeeze the juice of half a lemon and stir in.

Cover the pie plates with paste, fill with the mixture, and bake in a moderately hot oven

CURD CHEESE-CAKE.

246. One quart of milk,
 Half a pound of sugar,
 A quarter of a pound of butter,
 Five eggs,
 One tea spoonful of grated nutmeg,
 A quarter of a pound of currants.

Warm the milk, and turn it to a curd, with a piece of rennet, or a table spoonful of the wine in which a rennet has been soaked. As soon as the milk is a thick curd, take it out with a broad ladle or spoon, and lay it on a sieve to drain. Beat the eggs, and add the drained curd, also the sugar and butter, which must have been beaten to a cream, then the spice and fruit.

For those who would prefer it sweeter, more sugar may be added.

Line your pie plates with paste, fill them with the above mixture, and bake in a moderately hot oven.

COTTAGE CHEESE-CAKE.

247. One pint of curd,
 One gill and a half of cream,
 Three eggs,
 Sugar, nutmeg, and cinnamon to the taste.

Mix the curd and cream thoroughly together. Beat the eggs, add them with the sugar and spice.

Make a paste, cover your pie plates, and fill them with the mixture.

Bake in a moderate oven.

INDIAN FLORENDINES.

248. One quart of milk,
 Three eggs,
 One ounce of butter,
 Two table spoonsful of brandy,
 Sugar to the taste,
 As much Indian meal as will make the milk as thick as pap.

When the milk boils, stir in the Indian meal till it is thickened about like pap, then add the butter.

Set it off to cool. When cold stir in the eggs, which must have been well beaten, then the sugar and brandy.

They are very good without brandy.

Make a paste, cover your pie plates, pour in the above mixture, and bake in a moderate oven

RICE FLORENDINES.

249. One quart of milk,
 Eight eggs,
 Sugar to the taste,
 A quarter of a pound of butter,
 One tea spoonful of cinnamon,
 One tea spoonful of nutmeg,

Brandy, or rose-water to the taste,
Rice flour enough to thicken the milk.

—

Boil the milk, and stir in enough rice flour mixed with cold milk, to thicken it about as stiff as thick molasses. Add the butter while it is hot. Beat the eggs, stir them in when it gets cold, and add the other ingredients, bake in pie plates, with an under crust only.

—

ORANGE PUDDING.

250. Half a pound of butter,
Half a pound of sugar,
Five eggs,
Two table spoonsful of brandy,
The rind of an orange.

—

Lay the rind of an orange to soak over night. The next day boil it and mash it fine. It must be boiled in fresh water.

Beat the butter and sugar as for cake. Whisk the eggs and add to it, then stir in the liquor and orange.

Cover your pie plates with rich paste, fill them and bake in a moderate oven.

—

ALMOND PUDDING.

251. Half a pound of butter,
Half a pound of sugar,

Five eggs,
Six ounces of sweet almonds,
Two ounces of bitter almonds,
Half a gill of rose-water.

—

Blanch the almonds, pound them in a mortar to a paste with a little rose-water. Stir the butter and sugar to a cream. Whisk the eggs, mix all the ingredients together, line your pie plates with paste, fill them, and bake them as directed for other puddings.

COCOA-NUT PUDDING, No. 1.

252. A quarter of a pound of sugar,
A quarter of a pound of cocoa-nut,
Three ounces of butter,
The whites of six eggs,
Half a glass of wine and brandy mixed,
One table spoonful of rose-water.

—

Beat the butter and sugar smooth, whisk the eggs and add to it, then stir in the grated nut and liquor.

Cover your pie plates with rich crust, fill them with the mixture, and bake in a moderate oven.

COCOA-NUT PUDDING, No. 2.

253. Half a pound of sugar,
Half a pound of butter,

One pound of nut,
Eight eggs, the whites only,
Half a gill of wine and brandy mixed,
One table spoonful of rose-water.

Peel off the outer skin of the cocoa-nut, grate it and stir it into the butter and sugar, which must be beaten to a cream. Add the brandy, wine, and rose-water, then the whites of the eggs, which must be whisked till they are dry.

Bake in a puff paste.

APPLE PUDDING, No. 1.

254. Half a pound of the mashed apple,
Half a pound of butter,
Half a pound of sugar,
Five eggs,
Half a nutmeg,
Two table spoonsful of brandy, or rose-water if preferred.

Peel the apples and core them; cut them in small pieces, and stew them in very little water till they are soft. Pass them through a sieve to free them from lumps.

Beat the butter and sugar smooth, whisk the eggs and add to it; then stir in the apples, (which should be half a pound when mashed,) brandy or rose-water and nutmeg. Cover your pie plates with a rich crust and bake in a moderate oven.

These are very rich.

APPLE PUDDING, No. 2.

255. One pound of grated apple,
   Half a pound of butter,
   Half a pound of sugar,
   Six eggs,
   Half a pint of cream,
   The juice and grated rind of one lemon.

Grate your apples; beat the butter and sugar very light, whisk the eggs and add to it, add the apples, cream and lemon. Stir all together, line your pie plates with rich paste, pour in the mixture and bake it.

A few currants may be added.

PLAIN APPLE PUDDING, No. 3.

256. One pound of the mashed apples,
   A quarter of a pound of butter,
   Sugar to the taste,
   Six eggs,
   One tea spoonful of cinnamon,
   Half a nutmeg,
   Brandy or rose-water to the taste.

Peel the apples, cut them in slices, and stew

them in a very little water till they are tender. Mash them fine, and while they are hot add the butter. Set them away to cool. Beat the eggs, and when the apples are cold add the eggs and sugar, liquor and spice. Cover your pie plates with plain paste, fill them and bake in a moderate oven.

A quarter of a pound of dried currants may be added if preferred.

PUMPKIN PUDDING, No. 1.

257. A quarter of a pound of butter,
Sugar to the taste,
Eight eggs,
Two table spoonsful of brandy,
One tea spoonful of cinnamon,
One tea spoonful of grated nutmeg,
One pint of mashed pumpkin.

Stew the pumpkin in very little water, mash it fine, and add the butter to it whilst it is hot; whisk the eggs and stir into the pumpkin when it is cool enough, and add the other ingredients. Bake in a light paste.

PUMPKIN PUDDING, No. 2.

258. Eight eggs,
One pint of stewed pumpkin,
A quarter of a pound of butter,
A quarter of a pound of sugar,

Two table spoonsful of brandy,
One tea cupful of cream,
One tea spoonful of cinnamon,
One tea spoonful of nutmeg.

Stew the pumpkin in very little water, mash it very fine, add the butter and stand it away to cool. Beat the eggs, and when the pumpkin is cool add them and the other ingredients. Line your pie-plates with paste, pour in the pumpkin, and bake in a moderately hot oven.

When they are to be sent to the table sift sugar over them.

QUINCE PUDDING.

259. Six ounces of mashed quinces.
Half a pound of butter,
Half a pound of sugar,
Five eggs,
A table spoonful of brandy.

Stew the quinces, mash them very fine, and when nearly cold add to them the butter and sugar beaten to a cream. Whisk the eggs very light and stir in with the other ingredients. Cover your pie-plates with a nice paste, pour in the mixture and bake it.

FRENCH CUSTARD PUDDING.

260. One pint of milk,
One table-spoonful of flour,
Three eggs,
Sugar to the taste,
Flavored with rose-water, essence of lemon, or brandy.

Put on the milk to boil, mix the flour smoothly with a little cold milk; as soon as the milk boils stir in the mixture of flour and milk. Let it boil one minute, take it off and set away to cool. Beat the eggs, and when the milk is cool add them to it with the sugar, then the spice and rose-water, or whatever it is to be flavored with. Line your pie plates with paste, pour in the above mixture, and bake it in a moderate oven.

POTATO PUDDING.

261. Half a pound of butter,
Half a pound of sugar,
Half a pound of mashed potatoes,
Half a gill of cream,
Five eggs,
Two table spoonsful of brandy,
The grated peel of one orange,
One tea spoonful of nutmeg,
One tea spoonful of cinnamon.

Mash the boiled potatoes with the cream, and when cool, add to it the butter and sugar beaten to a cream, the eggs well whisked, and all the other ingredients. Bake in a puff paste.

SWEET POTATO PUDDING.

262. Made as the white potato.

CRANBERRY TARTS.

263. Stew your cranberries with sugar in the proportion of a pound of sugar to a pound of fruit, and merely enough water to melt the sugar. When they are done set them away to get cold. Make some shells of puff paste and fill with the fruit.

RHUBARB TARTS.

264. Cut your fruit in pieces, strew over it plenty of sugar, and stew it till it is soft, then mash it fine. Line your pie plates with good light paste, bake it, and when the shells are cold fill them with the stewed fruit.

RIPE PEACH PIE.

265. Pare your peaches, cut them in halves or quarters according to their size; lay them in a dish, and between every layer of peaches strew sugar according to the acidity of the peach. Line your pie plates with a paste, then put in the fruit and

cover with a lid of paste, leaving a small opening in the centre for the steam to escape.

Ripe peach pie may be made without any sugar; when the pie is baked take off the top crust, mash the fruit, and add as much sugar as will sweeten it. Be careful not to break the crust as it will disfigure the pie.

PEACH POT PIE.

266. Line the sides of a deep pot with a paste made in the proportion of half a pound of butter to one pound of flour. Then pare and slice some peaches, sugar them to your taste, and fill up the pot and cover the top with the paste, leaving an opening in the middle of the crust to permit the steam to escape while the pie is baking. Bake it in a moderately hot oven, and when cold serve it with cream.

QUINCE PIE.

267. The quinces are prepared in the same manner as for quince marmalade. Make your paste, line your pie plates, fill them with the marmalade, cover with a lid of paste and bake them.

Quince pies made in this way, are excellent during the winter when fruits are scarce.

PLUM PIE.

268. Cut your plums in two, and take out the

stones. Make a paste, line your pie plates, put in a layer of fruit and one of sugar, in the proportion of three-quarters of a pound of sugar to one pound of fruit. Roll out some paste, cover the pies and bake them in a moderate oven. Leave an opening in the centre of the lid to allow the steam to escape while they are baking.

QUINCE DUMPLINGS.

269. Pare and core your quinces, put them in a sauce-pan with very little water, and as soon as they *begin* to get tender take them out. Make a paste of six ounces of butter to a pound of flour, cover the fruit, tie them in dumpling cloths and boil them.

PEACH DUMPLINGS.

270. Choose large free-stone peaches; peel them, make a paste of six ounces of butter to one pound of flour; cover each peach with this paste, and boil them in cloths or nets till the fruit is tender. They are very nice. Serve with sugar and cream.

APPLE DUMPLINGS.

271. Make a paste of six ounces of butter to a pound of flour. Pare your apples, take out the cores, and cover them with the paste; tie them in

cloths and boil them till the apples are tender. Serve with sugar and cream, or molasses and butter.

CHERRY PIE.

272. Stew your cherries with sugar, in the proportion of a pound of cherries to half a pound of sugar, and stir in a little flour to thicken the syrup. Make a paste, as rich as you like, line your pie plates, fill with the fruit, and cover with a lid of the paste.

RHUBARB PIES.

273. Cut the young stalks in pieces about half an inch in length. Make a paste, cover the bottom of your pie plate, put in the fruit with a great deal of sugar, about four table spoonsful to each pie: put on a cover and bake them till the fruit is soft.

SWEET DISHES.

GUERNSEY PUDDING.

274. Half a pound of beef suet,
One pound of flour,
Half a pound of dried currants,
Half a pound of stoned raisins,
Two eggs,

Nutmeg and cinnamon to the taste,
Half a salt spoonful of salt.

Shred the suet, chop it fine, and rub it through the flour. Wash, pick, and dry the currants; seed the raisins, mix the currants and raisins together, and dredge over them as much flour as will adhere to them.

Beat the eggs till they are very thick and light, and add enough milk to form a batter—stir in the eggs, then the spices and salt, and lastly the fruit.

Dip your pudding bag into cold water, turn it wrong side out and flour it well, then turn it back again, pour in the batter, tie the mouth of the bag with a strong string, but take care to leave a space sufficient to allow the pudding to swell.

Have ready a pot of boiling water, with a plate in the bottom to prevent the bag from touching the bottom of the pot, put in the pudding and let it boil two hours and a half.

Keep a kettle of boiling water to fill up the pot as may be required. When the pudding is done, take it out of the pot, dip it for an instant in cold water, untie the bag, and turn it out on a dish.

To be eaten with sweet sauce.

EVE'S PUDDING.

275. Six eggs,
Six apples,

Six ounces of bread crumbs,
Six ounces of currants,
Six ounces of sugar,
Nutmeg to the taste,
Half a salt spoonful of salt.

Beat the eggs very light, add to them the apples, which must be finely chopped, the currants, sugar and bread crumbs, nutmeg and salt.

If the mixture should be too thick, add a little milk.

Pour the batter in a pan leaving a space at the top, tie a cloth tightly over the pan so as to exclude all the water, and let it boil three hours. Serve it with sweet sauce.

FRENCH PUDDING.

276. One quart of milk,
Ten table spoonsful of flour,
Eight eggs.

Beat the eggs very light, add them to the milk, with the flour. Butter a pan, pour in the mixture, and bake it. Serve it hot with sweet sauce.

SAGO PUDDING.

277. A quarter of a pound of sago,
Three pints of milk,

Eight eggs,
Sugar to the taste,
A quarter of a pound of butter,
Half a pound of currants,
Half a tea spoonful of nutmeg and cinnamon mixed.

Pick and wash the sago, and pour over it enough warm water to cover it. Put it in a warm place, and let it stand for three hours to soak.

Wash, pick, and dry your currants, and sift flour over them.

Boil the sago in the milk until it is completely incorporated with it. Add the butter and stand it away to cool. Beat the eggs, and stir them into the milk; add the sugar, fruit, and spice.

Butter a deep dish, pour in the mixture and bake it.

FRENCH BREAD PUDDING.

278. One-half of a four cent baker's loaf,
One quart of milk,
Three eggs,
One gill of dried currants,
Sugar to the taste.

Boil the milk, slice the bread, and pour the boiling milk over it. Stand it away to cool.

Beat the eggs, and add them and the sugar when

the milk is cool. Wash, pick and flour the currants, and stir them in to the mixture. Put it in a pudding dish, and bake it half an hour in a moderate oven. Serve it with or without sweet sauce.

GREEN CORN PUDDING.

279. Cut off the cob one dozen ears of green corn whilst in the milky state. Beat five eggs very light, add to them one quart of milk, with sugar to the taste, stir in the grains of corn, butter thoroughly the bottom and sides of a pudding pan, pour in the mixture, and bake it in a very moderate oven for three hours. It may be eaten with any kind of sweet sauce; or the sugar may be left out of the pudding, and then it may be eaten hot for breakfast with butter.

RICE CUP PUDDINGS.

280. Pick and wash a tea cupful of rice, and boil it in a quart of milk till it is very thick and dry; add to this whilst it is hot, a pint of rich milk or cream, and two ounces of butter. When it is sufficiently cool, add three eggs, well beaten, and sugar to the taste. Butter your cups, pour in the mixture, and bake in a moderate oven. Grate nutmeg over the top, and serve them with cream.

NEWCASTLE PUDDING.

281. Make a custard of six eggs to a quart of

milk and sugar to the taste. Beat the eggs; stir them in the milk, and add the sugar. Butter some bread, lay it in the bottom of a dish, then strew over it some currants, then another layer of buttered bread and currants. Pour on the egg and milk prepared as above, and bake it until the custard is thick.

PEACH BAKED PUDDING.

282. Line a deep pudding dish with slices of baker's bread cut thin. Fill up the dish with ripe peaches cut in pieces and sugared, cover the top with some bread sliced thin, buttered and dipped in the yelk of an egg well beaten. Set the pudding in the oven and bake it. Serve it with milk or cream.

FARMER'S APPLE PUDDING.

283. Stew some tender apples; if the apples are juicy they will require very little water to cook them; add to one pound of the mashed apple, whilst it is hot, a quarter of a pound of butter, and sugar to the taste. Beat four eggs and stir in when the apple is cold.

Butter the bottom and sides of a deep pudding dish, strew it very thickly with bread crumbs, put in the mixture, and strew bread crumbs plentifully over the top. Set it in a tolerably hot oven, and when baked, sift sugar over.

This is good with a glass of rich milk.

It is a good substitute for pie, and can be eaten by those who cannot partake of pastry.

RICE PUDDING, No. 1.

284. Half a tea cup of rice,
Two ounces of butter,
Three pints of milk.
Five eggs,
Sugar to the taste.

Put the rice and milk together, and simmer it gently till the rice is soft, then take it out and add the butter while the rice is hot. Set it away to cool. Beat the eggs, stir them in when the rice is cool, and add the sugar. Put the mixture in a pudding dish, place it in a moderate oven, and as soon as it forms a custard take it out.

Grate nutmeg over the top.

RICE PUDDING, No. 2.

285. One quart of milk,
Rice flour enough to thicken the milk,
Six eggs,
Two ounces of butter,
Sugar to the the taste.

Boil the milk and thicken it with rice flour mixed with cold milk. It should be about as thick as pap.

Add the butter while the milk is hot. When cool add the beaten eggs, and sugar to the taste.

Put it in a deep dish and bake it till a fine custard is formed.

Dried currants may be added before it is baked, also a little lemon or rose-water.

BOILED RICE PUDDING.

286. Pick and wash your rice, tie it in a pudding bag, allowing it room to swell. Boil it till the rice is soft, and serve it with sugar and cream, or molasses and butter.

RICE PUDDING WITH FRUIT.

287. Put your rice in a stew-pan, with very little milk; that is, to one cup of rice one gill of milk. Stand it where it will be hot, but not boil; when the rice has absorbed all the milk add to it a quarter of a pound of dried currants, and one egg, well beaten. Boil it in a bag till the rice is tender, and serve it with sugar and cream.

More fruit may be added to the rice if it should be preferred.

RICE CUPS.

288. Boil some rice in very little milk so as it may be perfectly dry when done. Mash it fine, and while it is hot add a little butter and sugar to

the taste. Put the rice in cups; you should fill them as full as they will hold, by pressing the rice into them. When they are cold, turn them out on a dish, pour a custard round them, and eat them with cream.

PLUM PUDDING.

289. One quart of milk,
Six eggs,
A quarter of a pound of seeded raisins,
A quarter of a pound of currants,
Sugar to the taste.

Beat the eggs, and add them to the milk with the fruit. Pour it in a pudding dish, cover the top with slices of bread well buttered. First dip the bread in the milk, so as it may be brown when it is baked.

This is generally eaten cold. It may be flavored with lemon or vanilla.

BOILED PUDDING, No. 1.

290. Pour over a pint of the crumbs of baker's bread as much boiling milk as will moisten it, mash it smoothly in the milk. Beat the yelks of four eggs and add them to the bread and milk, beat it very hard; then whisk the whites of the eggs and stir in gently with as much flour as will make a batter. Fruit may be added if preferred, but the

pudding will be lighter without. Rinse your pudding bag, flour it on the inside, pour in the batter, tie it very closely, leaving room for it to swell. Boil it two hours.

BOILED PUDDING, No. 2.

291. Eight eggs,
   One quart of milk,
   One pint of flour,
   Salt just to taste.

Beat the eggs very light, the yelks and whites separate—the yelks should be as thick as batter—add to them the flour and milk alternately, and very gradually, beating it hard all the time; then stir in the whites, but do not beat it after they are in. The whites should be very dry. Wet your pudding bag, wring it dry, flour the inside, and pour in the pudding. It requires one hour to boil, and is very delicate, being very little thicker than a custard. Serve it with any kind of sweet sauce. This makes a light wholesome pudding.

INDIAN BOILED PUDDING.

292. One quart of milk,
   Four eggs,
   Half a pound of dried currants,
   Two ounces of butter,

Salt just to taste,
Indian meal sufficient to form a batter.

—

Stand the butter near the fire where it will dissolve without getting hot. Stir as much Indian meal in the milk as will form a thick batter, then add the salt and melted butter. Separate the yelks and whites of the eggs; beat the yelks very thick and light, and add to the batter; whisk the whites till they are very dry, stir them gently into the mixture. Have your currants washed, picked and dried, flour them and stir in at the last.

Dip your pudding bag in water, wring it out, turn it wrong side out, flour it well, turn it again, pour in the mixture and tie it closely with a strong string, taking care to leave room at the top of the bag for the pudding to swell.

Have ready a pot of boiling water, put the pudding in, and have a kettle of boiling water to fill it up as it boils away. Keep the pudding boiling all the time, as it would be heavy if it should cease. Let it boil three hours. When done immerse the bag for an instant into a pan of cold water, untie the string, turn back the bag and place your pudding on a dish. Serve it immediately.

To be eaten with any kind of sweet sauce.

———

INDIAN BAKED PUDDING.

293. One pint of Indian meal,

One heaping table spoonful of wheat flour,
A table spoonful of butter,
Four eggs,
Salt just to taste,
Milk enough to form a batter.

Stand your butter near the fire to warm, add it to the Indian meal, then the salt and milk. Beat the eggs very light, the yelks and whites separate; add the yelks to the Indian batter, then the whites alternately with the flour. Do not beat it after the whites are in. Butter a pan, pour in the batter, and bake it in a moderate oven.

This pudding is very good with a quarter of a pound of currants and a quarter of a pound of raisins, floured and stirred into the batter.

To be served with sweet sauce of any kind.

OXFORD PUDDING.

294. Half a pint of bread crumbs,
One pint of milk,
Six eggs,
Two ounces of butter,
Half a pint of cream,
A quarter of a pound of dried currants,
Sugar and nutmeg to the taste.

After the bread is soaked in the milk, which should be warm, mash it very smooth and add the butter while it is hot. Beat the eggs very light, the yelks first, and stir them into the bread and milk, then add the cream, sugar, nutmeg and fruit. Lastly have the whites whisked to a dry froth; stir them gently into the mixture; butter your cups, half fill them with the batter, and bake them in a tolerably hot oven. Serve with pudding sauce.

COLLEGE PUDDING.

295. Four eggs,
   One pint of milk,
   A little salt,
   Flour to make a rather thin batter,
   One dessert spoonful of dissolved carbonate of ammonia.

Beat the yelks of the eggs very light, add the salt, milk and flour. The batter must not be thick. Beat the whole very hard for ten or fifteen minutes. Then stir in gently the whites of the egg, which should have been whisked very dry. Do not beat the batter after the whites are in, only stir it sufficiently to incorporate them with it. Lastly add the ammonia. Butter well a cake mould or iron pan, pour in the mixture and bake it in an oven about as hot as for bread.

This pudding is very nice with wine or lemon sauce. Cream sauce may be served with it if preferred.

BLANC MANGE.

296. One pint of milk,
One pint of cream,
One ounce of isinglass,
The grated rind and juice of one lemon,
Sugar to the taste.

Boil the milk and pour it whilst hot over the isinglass, let it stand near the fire until it is perfectly dissolved, then strain it through a flannel jelly bag into the pint of cream, to which add the grated rind and juice of one lemon, and sugar to the taste. Let the whole boil once; take it off the fire, strain it again through your jelly bag, and pour it in moulds. Set it in a cool place.

CLEAR BLANC MANGE.

297. Boil four calves' feet in three quarts of water until the water is reduced to one quart, then strain it through a flannel jelly bag and stand it away to cool. When it is perfectly cold scrape off all the fat, which will be congealed in a cake on the top; after you have scraped all off as clean as you can get it, take a piece of clean damp sponge, or soft cloth a little damp, and wipe the top of the jelly and the inner edge of the vessel which contains it, lest any of the grease should be combined with the jelly when it is melted, as it would destroy its transparency. Break the jelly in pieces, put it

in a preserving pan, add to it one pound of pulverized white sugar, half an ounce of bitter almonds pounded in a mortar with a little rose-water; put the almonds in the mortar one at a time, so as to pound them very finely, they should be like cream when done; strain them and add them to the jelly with a table spoonful of rose-water. Place the preserving pan in a vessel of boiling water, let it stand till it gets *very hot*, but do not let it boil. Strain it through the jelly bag several times, and when perfectly clear pour it in moulds; wet them inside first to prevent the jelly from adhering to them, and stand them in a cold place. When you strain the jelly do not squeeze the bag, as by that means you force the sediment through it; and by no means wash it, as it is impossible to wring it perfectly dry, and consequently the jelly will be thinned; scrape it on the inside as clean as you can each time.

CHARLOTTE DE RUSSE.

298. Get a sponge cake which has been baked in a mould, and weighing about two pounds or little more. Place this in the centre of a deep china or glass dish. Mix together half a pint of wine with half a pint of water, and sweeten it well with white sugar. Pour this over the cake, which should have been baked the day before; let it stand till it has absorbed as much of the wine as it will take

up, then make a custard according to the following directions: Put over the fire three half-pints of milk, well sweetened and flavored with lemon or vanilla, and as soon as it is ready to boil stir in *very* gradually the yelks of six eggs which should have been well beaten. As soon as the milk and egg begins to bubble a little at the edges, take it off the fire. When the custard is lukewarm pour it round the cake in the dish; whisk the whites of the eggs to a stiff, dry froth, sweeten them with powdered white sugar and flavor with essence of lemon or lemon juice. Pile the whites on the top of the cake and serve it immediately.

PEACH CHARLOTTE.

299. Line the bottom and sides of a dish with slices of fresh sponge cake. Pare some ripe peaches, cut them in halves, sprinkle sugar over them, and fill up the dish. Then whisk a pint of sweetened cream; as the froth rises, take it off till all is done. Pile the cream on the top of the peaches and send it to the table.

SAVOY CHARLOTTE.

300. Lay some slices of sponge cake in the bottom of a deep dish; moisten it with wine. Make a custard of one quart of milk and five eggs, with as much sugar as will sweeten it. Beat the eggs, stir them into the milk with the sugar, pour

it in a pan, place the pan in a vessel of water, put it in the oven, and as soon as the custard is thick, set it away to cool. With a silver spoon lay the custard over the cake. Take half a pint of cream, flavor it with wine and white sugar, whip it to a froth, and as the froth rises, take it off carefully and lay it on the custard.

The wine may be dispensed with, and the charlotte be very nice, if made according to the above directions.

CHERRY CHARLOTTE.

301. Stone and stew some morella cherries; to each pound of cherries add three-quarters of a pound of sugar, and one tea spoonful of flour, mixed smoothly with a little water. When the fruit is done, butter some baker's bread, lay it on a dish, spread some of the stewed fruit over it, then put another layer of bread and fruit; cover the top with the fruit.

This is very nice served with cream.

RICE MILK.

302. Two quarts of milk,
Two gills of rice,
Sugar to the taste.

Pick and wash the rice, put it in the milk, and set it over a slow fire to boil.

When the rice is *very* soft, add sugar to the taste, pour it into a bowl, and stand it away to cool.

Grate nutmeg on the top.

RICE FLUMMERY.

303. One quart of milk,
   One ounce of butter,
   Sugar to the taste,
   Rice flour enough to thicken the milk.

As soon as the milk begins to boil, stir in as much rice flour as will make it as thick as a stiff batter.

Add the butter and sugar, turn it out in cups, and stand it away to get cold.

Serve it with cream and nutmeg if preferred.

It would be better to place the vessel in which the milk is to be boiled in a pan of hot water, which will prevent the milk from burning, should the fire be hot.

APPLE FLOATING ISLAND.

304. Stew in a sauce-pan, with very little water, eight or nine fine apples; when they are soft, pass them through a sieve, and season them with nutmeg and pulverized sugar to the taste. Whisk to a froth the whites of four or five eggs, mix them gradually with the apples; stir in one

table spoonful of rose-water. Sweeten some cream or rich milk, and place the above mixture upon it in heaps.

This is a very nice dish.

FLOATING ISLAND.

305. One quart of milk,
Sugar to the taste,
The whites of three eggs.

Sweeten the milk to your taste, and to it add wine, if you prefer it. Then whisk the whites of the eggs to a dry froth, and to every egg add one tea spoonful of currant, quince, or any kind of jelly you choose, add also one tea spoonful of white sugar to each white.

Pile the froth upon the milk, and serve it soon, as the whites will fall.

WHIPS.

306. The whites of three eggs,
Sugar to the taste,
One pint of milk or cream.

Mix the whites of the egg (without beating them) into the milk. Sweeten it to your taste, then whisk it to a froth, which must be taken off and put in glasses as it rises. The milk may be flavored with lemon or vanilla.

SYLLABUB.

307. Half a pound of sugar,
Three pints of lukewarm milk or cream,
One tea cupful of wine.

Dissolve the sugar in the wine, then pour in the milk, in a small stream, from a vessel, holding it up very high so as to cause the milk to froth. In the country it is best to milk into the bowl, the last of the milk which is taken from the cow is richer.

VANILLA CUP CUSTARDS.

308. Pound a vanilla bean in a mortar, and stir it into three pints of milk, eight well beaten eggs, and sugar to the taste.

Fill your cups, place them in a pan of hot water, set them in the oven, and as soon as a custard is formed take them out.

They are very nice if placed on the ice in warm weather an hour or two before they are served.

HASTY PUDDING, OR FARMER'S RICE.

309. Beat one egg very light, and add to it as much flour as it will moisten. Rub it through your hands until the flour is in fine dry lumps like bread crumbs.

Put on a quart of milk to boil, and when boiling, stir in as much of this flour as will make it very thick. Serve it with butter and sugar, and rich cream if you have it.

SPANISH FRITTERS.

310. Cut the soft part of bakers' bread in slices a quarter of an inch thick, and of any form you choose. Take a pint of milk or cream, three well beaten eggs, half a tea spoonful of nutmeg and cinnamon mixed, three drops of the essence of lemon, and sugar to the taste, stir all well together and pour over the pieces of bread. When they have absorbed as much of the milk as they will, take them out before they get too soft, and fry them of a nice light brown on both sides.

They may be served with or without sweet sauce.

APPLE FRITTERS.

311.. One pint of milk,
 Three eggs,
 Salt just to taste,
 As much flour as will make a batter.

Beat the yelks and whites separately, add the yelks to the milk, stir in the whites with as much flour as will make a batter; have ready some tender apples, peel them, cut them in slices round the apple; take the core carefully out of the centre of each slice, and to every spoonful of batter lay in a slice of the apple, which must be cut very thin—fry them in hot lard of a light brown on both sides.

ORANGE FRITTERS.

312. These are made as the above, only a slice of orange is to be substituted for the apple.

GERMAN PUFFS.

313. One pint of milk,
   Three eggs,
   One pound of flour,
   One dessert spoonful of *dissolved* salæratus,
   A tea spoonful of butter,
   A salt spoon of salt.

Beat the yelks and whites of the eggs separately. The yelks must be as thick as batter, and the whites perfectly dry.

Add to the yelks half the milk and half the flour, stir it well until the batter is smooth, then add the remainder of the flour and milk.

Warm the butter and stir in and beat the batter thus made till it is light and full of bubbles.

Stir in the salæratus, and lastly the whites—but do not beat it after the whites have been added, as that will make it tough.

Butter tea cups, or an earthen mould, pour in the batter, and bake it in a moderate oven.

Serve with butter and sugar, or any kind of sauce which may be preferred.

They require from half an hour to three-quarters to bake.

SNOW CUSTARD.

314. One quart of milk,
   Eight eggs,
   One vanilla bean, or a little grated lemon peel.

Beat the eggs, leaving out the whites of four, add them to the milk. Pound the vanilla bean in a mortar, and mix it with the milk. Pour the whole in your pudding dish, place it in a pan of boiling water, and when the custard is thick set it away to cool.

About fifteen minutes before it is to be served, beat the whites to a dry froth, sweeten with fine white sugar, pile it on the top and send it to the table. If suffered to stand the white of egg will fall.

BOILED CUSTARD.

315. Eight eggs,
   One quart of milk,
   Sugar to the taste.

Add the sugar to the milk with any thing to flavor it you choose. Set it over the fire, and as soon as it begins to boil stir in the beaten eggs very gradually—stir all the time one way; as soon as it is thick take it off the fire, or it will curdle. Fill your cups and stand it away to cool. Grate nutmeg over before they are sent to table.

BAKED PEARS.

316. Wash them, put them in a deep pan, strew over plenty of white or brown sugar, and pour very little water in the bottom of the pan. Put them in a moderate oven and let them cook slowly till the fruit is soft. Serve them with cream.

STEWED CHERRIES.

317. Stone some cherries, and to every pound of fruit add half a pound of sugar. When they are done set them away to get cold. Serve them with cream.

BAKED APPLES.

318. Wash the apples, take out the cores, and put them in a deep pan; strew sugar over them, and bake them in a cool oven till they are soft. Serve them with cream.

A piece of lemon peel may be stuck in the centre of each apple before it is set in the oven.

BLACKBERRY MUSH.

319. Put your fruit in a preserving kettle, mash

it to a pulp, with sugar enough to make it quite sweet. Set it over the fire, and as it begins to simmer stir in very gradually two tea spoonsful of flour to a quart of fruit. It should be stirred all the time it is boiling. Serve it either warm or cold, with cream.

Raspberries may be cooked in the same way.

RICE DUMPLINGS.

320. Put your rice in a stew-pan, and pour on each cup of rice one gill of milk; stand it near the fire where it will keep hot but not boil. As soon as it has absorbed all the milk, pare your apples, take out the cores, and put the rice around them instead of paste. Boil them until the apple is soft.

They should be tied in dumpling cloths.

GLAZED CURRANTS.

321. Select large ripe bunches of currants, wash them by dipping them in a bowl of cold water, and drain them dry; have ready the whites of two eggs, give them three or four beats, dip the bunches in the egg, place them on a sieve so as not to touch each other, sift powdered sugar over them and place them in a warm place to dry. The whites of the eggs should only be broken, but not beaten till dry, or they will not adhere to the fruit.

GLAZED STRAWBERRIES

322. Choose large ripe strawberries, pick them off the vines so as the stems may all adhere to the fruit. Dip them one at a time in a vessel of cold water and place them on a sieve to dry. Beat the whites of two or three eggs, according to the quantity of fruit. The egg should be beaten very little or it will not adhere to the fruit, dip the berries in the egg one at a time, place them on a sieve so as not to touch each other, and sift powdered white sugar over them. They are very ornamental to a dessert table. Bunches of grapes, oranges peeled and quartered, or any small fruit may be done in the same manner.

STEWED RIPE PEACHES.

323. Take ripe peaches, cut them in half, and to every pound of fruit allow half a pound of sugar, and half a wine-glass of water. Peel your peaches, sprinkle the sugar over them, and stew them till tender. Stand them away to cool and serve them with cream.

COLD CUSTARD.

324. Sweeten to your taste, one quart of milk with white sugar; stir into it a table spoonful of wine in which a rennet has been soaked; if this does not flavor the milk sufficiently add some more wine without the rennet; or, if the use of wine is

an objection, the rennet may be soaked in water. In warm weather one hour before it is to be served will be the proper time to make it, as it is not good if the curd is hard. As soon as the rennet is put into the milk stir it and pour it in cups to coagulate. Or you may serve it in a glass bowl. It is to be eaten with cream.

It may be made as above directed, without the sugar, and served with sweetened cream and grated nutmeg.

APPLE CREAM.

325. Stew half a dozen tender apples, mash them to a pulp; whisk the whites of six eggs till they are very light, and as soon as the apples are cold add them to the eggs with five ounces of pulverized loaf sugar. Whisk the whole till it will stand up when placed on a dish.

Serve it with sweetened cream flavored with lemon, vanilla, or wine.

TEA CAKE.

SHORT CAKES.

326. Half a pound of butter,
A pound of flour; cold water to form a dough.

Cut up the butter in the flour, and rub it until they are thoroughly mixed. Roll the dough out in sheets, and cut the cakes with a cutter or tumbler. Serve them hot, split them open, and eat them with butter.

MUFFINS.

327. Four eggs,
   One quart of milk,
   Two ounces of butter,
   One gill of yeast,
   Salt just to taste,
   Enough flour to make a batter.

Warm the milk and butter, beat the eggs and stir in the milk, then add flour enough to make a thick batter, add the yeast and set it to rise.

Butter your bake-iron and the inside of your muffin-rings, place the rings on the iron and fill them three parts full of the batter. The iron should not be too hot or they will not be done through. Split or tear them open, butter them, and send them to the table hot.

HARD BISCUITS.

328. Four pounds of flour,
   Three ounces of butter,
   Four eggs,
   Salt to taste,
   Milk enough to form a dough.

Take out a tea cupful of the flour and set it aside. To the remainder add the butter cut up small, the eggs well beaten, a little salt, and milk enough to form a dough. Knead the dough well, then roll it out, sprinkle over it a portion of the reserved flour, roll it out again and sprinkle on more flour till all the flour is used. Roll it out thin, cut out your cakes, and bake in a moderate oven.

YORKSHIRE BISCUITS.

329. Three pounds of flour,
  One gill of yeast,
  A quarter of a pound of butter,
  Three eggs,
  Milk enough to form a dough.

Rub the butter and flour together. Beat the eggs and add them, then the yeast and milk to form a dough. Stand it away to rise, when light make it out in biscuits, butter your tins, place the biscuits on them, let them rise again and bake them.

POTATO ROLLS.

330. Four large potatoes boiled,
  One table spoonful of butter,
  Salt to the taste,
  Half a pint of milk,

Half a tea cupful of yeast,
Flour sufficient to form a dough.

—

Boil the potatoes, peel and mash them, and while they are hot add the butter and salt, then pour in the milk. When the mixture is lukewarm add the yeast and flour. Knead the dough, set it away to rise, when it is light mould out your rolls, place them on buttered tins, let them rise and bake them.

BRENTFORD ROLLS.

331. Two pounds of flour,
Two ounces of powdered sugar,
A quarter of a pound of butter,
Two eggs,
One gill of yeast,
Milk enough to form a dough,
Salt to taste.

—

Rub the flour, butter and sugar together; beat the eggs and add with the other ingredients. When light, mould the dough out in rolls, let them rise again, and bake them on tins.

FRENCH ROLLS.

332. One ounce of butter,
One pound of flour,
One gill of home-made yeast,

One egg,
Milk enough to make a dough.

Rub the butter through the flour, beat the egg and stir in, then add the yeast, milk, and a little salt. Knead the dough, when it is light mould it out into large biscuits, and bake them on tins.

PARSNIP CAKE.

333. Boil your parsnips till perfectly soft; pass them through a colander. To one tea cupful of mashed parsnip add one quart of warm milk, with a quarter of a pound of butter dissolved in it, a little salt, and one gill of yeast, with flour enough to make a thick batter. Set it away to rise, which will require several hours. When light stir in as much flour as will make a dough, knead it well and let it rise again. Make it out in cakes about a quarter or half an inch thick, butter your tins or pans, put them on and set them to rise. As soon as they are light bake them in a very hot oven. When done wash over the tops with a little water, and send them to the table hot.

These biscuits do not taste of the parsnips.

MARYLAND BISCUITS.

334. One pound of flour,
One ounce of butter,

As much luke-warm milk as will wet the flour.
Salt just to taste.

Rub the butter and flour together thoroughly, add the salt, and lastly just enough milk to form a *very stiff* dough; knead the dough, then pound it with a rolling-pin. Break the dough in pieces, pound and knead it again, and so on for two or three hours. It will be very smooth and light when kneaded sufficiently.

Make it out in small biscuits and bake in a moderate oven.

WAFFLES.

335. Two eggs,
   One pint of milk,
   Half an ounce of butter,
   Half a gill of yeast,
   Salt just to taste,
   As much flour as will form a thick batter.

Warm the milk and butter together; beat the eggs and add them by turns with the flour; stir in the yeast and salt. When they are light, heat your waffle-irons and butter them; pour in some of the batter and brown them on both sides. Butter them and serve them with or without sugar and cinnamon.

WAFFLES WITHOUT YEAST.

336. Three eggs,
   One pint of milk,
   One tea spoonful of butter,
   As much flour as will make a batter.

Beat the yelks and whites separately. Melt the butter, and while lukewarm stir it into the milk. Whisk the yelks very light, add to them the milk and flour alternately, beat it well, lastly stir in the whites, which must be whisked very dry. The batter should not be beaten after the whites are in.

Grease your waffle-irons after having heated them, fill them nearly full of the batter, close them and place them over the fire—turn the irons so as to bake the waffle on both sides—when done take it out and butter it.

These must be baked the moment they are mixed.

BUCKWHEAT CAKES.

337. One pint of buckwheat meal,
   One quart of water,
   Salt just to taste,
   One gill of home-made yeast.

Mix the water (which should be lukewarm if the weather is cold,) with the meal, add the salt and yeast, beat it well; when light bake them on a griddle. Grease the griddle, pour on a little of the batter, spread it so as to form a cake about the size of a breakfast plate. The cakes should be very smooth at the edges. When they are done on one side turn them, when brown on both sides, put some butter on the plate, place the cake on it, butter the top, bake another and put on it, butter it and send them to the table.

Buckwheat cakes are much better if they are sent to the table with only one or two on a plate.

RYE BATTER CAKES

338. One pint of rye meal; to this add enough lukewarm milk to make a thin batter, a little salt just to taste. Beat it well—add a gill of home-made yeast.

When they are light, bake them on a griddle as buckwheat cakes.

GUERNSEY BUNS.

339. One pound of flour,
A quarter of a pound of butter,
One gill of yeast.

Cut up the butter in the flour and rub it well together. Then add the yeast and as much milk as will form a dough. Let it rise, then make it out in cakes, grease tins or pans, and lay the buns on them; as soon as they rise again bake them in a quick oven.

TOTTENHAM MUFFINS.

340. One quart of flour,
   Three eggs,
   One gill of yeast,
   A table spoonful of butter,
   Salt to taste,
   Milk sufficient to form a batter.

Place the butter near the fire where it may dissolve but not get hot.

Beat the eggs till they are thick, add them to the flour, with as much milk as will make a thick batter; stir in the melted butter and salt. Lastly a gill of yeast. Bake in muffin hoops.

CRUMPETS OR FLANNEL CAKES.

341. One pint of milk,
   One egg,
   A tea spoonful of butter,
   Salt to taste,
   Half a gill of yeast,
   As much wheat flour as will form a batter.

Warm the milk and butter together; it should be lukewarm but not hot. Beat up the egg and add to it with the salt, then flour enough to form a batter; lastly the yeast. Set it to rise, and when light grease your bake-iron and bake them like buckwheat cakes—butter them and serve them hot.

SCOTCH CRUMPETS.

342. Two eggs,
  One pint of milk,
  A tea spoonful of butter,
  Half a gill of yeast,
  Salt to taste,
  As much oatmeal or unbolted flour as will make a batter.

Warm the butter in the milk—it must be merely lukewarm when the eggs are put in. Beat the eggs very light, stir them into the milk, and add as much oatmeal or unbolted flour (the latter is preferable,) as will form a batter, add the salt and yeast, beat it well, and stand it away to rise.

Bake them like buckwheat cakes, butter them and serve hot.

INDIAN FRITTERS.

343. Two tea cupsful of Indian meal,
  Half a tea-cup of wheat flour,
  Salt just to taste,
  Three eggs,
  Milk enough to form a thick batter.

Mix the Indian meal and salt, stir into this as much milk as will make a thick batter. Whisk the yelks very thick and light and stir into the Indian; then beat the whites to a stiff dry froth, and stir them into the mixture alternately with the flour. Do not beat it after the white is in as that will make it tough.

Have a pan with some hot lard, drop a spoonful of the batter into it, and bake a light brown on both sides. They should be baked as soon as they are mixed, as if suffered to stand they will be heavy.

With a sweet sauce these may be eaten as dessert.

INDIAN SLAPPERS.

344. One pint of Indian meal,
One gill of boiling milk,
One tea spoonful of butter,
Salt just to taste,
One gill of wheat flour,
Two eggs,
One gill of yeast,
Milk sufficient to make a batter.

Cut up the butter in the Indian meal, and add the salt, then stir into it the gill of boiling milk. Beat the eggs, and when the meal is cool add them and the wheat flour to it, with as much milk as will form a batter. Then add the yeast. When the batter is light grease your griddle, and bake them as buckwheat cakes.

INDIAN PONE.

345. Put on one quart of water in a pot, as soon as it boils stir in as much Indian meal as will make a *very thin* batter. Beat it frequently whilst it is boiling, which will require ten minutes. Then take it off, pour it in a pan, and add one ounce of butter, and salt to the taste.

When the batter is lukewarm stir in as much Indian meal as will make it quite thick.

Set it away to rise in the evening; in the morning make it out in small cakes, butter your tins and bake in a moderate oven. Or the more common way is to butter pans, fill them three parts full, and bake them.

This cake requires no yeast.

JOHNNY OR JOURNEY CAKE.

346. One quart of Indian meal, add to this salt to taste, and pour over it as much boiling water as will form a dough.

Take the dough, roll it into balls, press it on a board to form the cake—it should be about the eighth of an inch in thickness. Place the board in front of the fire so as the heat may brown the cakes, turn them, and when brown on both sides, send them to the table.

INDIAN LIGHT CAKE.

347. One pint of Indian meal,
   One pint of milk,
   Two eggs,
   One tea spoonful of butter,
   Salt to the taste,
· One tea spoonful of *dissolved* salæratus.

Mix the butter and salt with the meal; boil half the milk, add the *dissolved* salæratus and the eggs, after they have been well beaten, to the remaining half of cold milk. Pour the boiling milk over the meal and let it cool. Then add the cold milk and salæratus. Bake it in a shallow pan.

INDIAN MUFFINS, No. 1.

348. One pint of Indian meal,
   One pint of wheat meal,
   Two eggs,
   One gill of yeast,
   Salt to the taste,
   As much milk as will make a batter.

Pour as much boiling milk over the Indian meal as will wet it. Beat the eggs very light and add them alternately with the cold milk and flour. Lastly stir in the yeast and salt.

They may be baked in pans or rings, as soon as they rise.

INDIAN MUFFINS, No. 2

349. One quart of corn meal,
Half a gill of yeast,
Two eggs,
Salt to the taste,
Half an ounce of butter.

Cut up the butter into the meal, and pour on it enough boiling milk to form a thick batter; set it away to cool. Whisk the eggs very light and add to the batter, then the yeast and salt.

Butter square tins, fill them three parts full, and bake in a quick oven. Or they may be baked in rings as wheat muffins.

INDIAN MEAL BREAKFAST CAKES.

350. One quart of Indian meal,
Two eggs,
A tea spoonful of *dissolved* salæratus,
Half an ounce of butter,
Salt to taste,
Milk sufficient to make a thick batter.

Beat the eggs very thick and light. Cut up the

butter in the meal, then pour over it enough boiling water to wet it. When it is cool add the eggs and salt; pour the dissolved salæratus into the milk, and add as much milk as will make it into a thick batter.

Butter square tin pans, fill them but about two-thirds and bake in a quick oven. When done cut them into squares and serve hot.

MILK BISCUITS.

351. A quarter of a pound of butter,
One quart of milk,
One gill of yeast,
As much flour as will form the dough,
A little salt.

Stir flour into the milk so as to form a very thick batter, and add the yeast, this is called a sponge. This should be done in the evening; in the morning cut up the butter, and set it near the fire where it will dissolve but not get hot; pour the melted butter into the sponge, then stir in enough flour to form a dough, knead it well and stand it away to rise. As soon as it is perfectly light, butter your tins, make out the dough in small cakes, and let them rise. When they are light bake them in a *very* quick oven, take them out, wash the tops over with water and send them to the table hot.

SALLY LUNN, No. 1.

352. Two pounds of flour,
Half a pound of butter,
Three eggs,
One pint of milk,
Half a gill of yeast,
Salt to taste.

Cut up the butter in the flour, and with your hands rub it well together. Beat the eggs and add them gradually to the flour alternately with the milk. Stir in the yeast and salt.

Bake it in an earthen mould or iron pan one hour.

SALLY LUNN, No. 2.

353. A quarter of a pound of butter,
A pound of flour,
Two eggs,
Salt to taste,
Half a gill of yeast,
Milk to make a soft dough.

Cut up the butter and warm it in a little milk; when the milk is lukewarm stir it into the flour with the eggs beaten light, and the yeast. Butter your cake mould, and set it near the fire to rise. When perfectly light bake it in a moderate oven.

It is always eaten hot.

WATER TOAST.

354. Toast some slices of bread, pound the crust to soften it, butter it well on both sides: have a vessel of boiling water with a little salt in it. On each slice of bread put one table spoonful of the boiling water. Serve it hot.

MILK TOAST.

355. Slice some bread, toast it of a nice light brown on both sides. Boil a pint of milk; mix together two tea spoonsful of flour in a little cold water; stir this into the boiling milk. Let it boil about one minute, then add a little salt and stir into it two ounces of butter. Dip the toast in the milk, place it on a dish, and pour the remainder of the milk over it.

The toast may be made much richer by increasing the quantity of butter.

MUSH CAKES.

356. One quart of milk,
   A quarter of a pound of butter,
   Half a pint of yeast,
   Salt to taste,
   Indian meal sufficient to thicken the milk,
   Flour enough to make a dough.

Boil the milk, and stir into it as much Indian meal mixed with cold milk as will make a mush as thick as batter, add the butter and salt while the mush is hot. As soon as it becomes lukewarm stir in the yeast and as much flour as will form a dough; cover it and stand it to rise. When light make it out into biscuits, put them in buttered pans, and as soon as they rise again bake them in a hot oven. These cakes are very nice.

RICE WAFFLES.

357. One gill of rice,
Three gills of flour,
Salt just to taste,
One ounce of butter,
Three eggs,
As much milk as will make it a thick batter.

Boil the rice in very little water until it is soft; drain it and mash it fine. Then add the butter to the rice whilst it is warm; whisk the eggs very light, the yelks and whites separately, add the yelks to the rice, and as much milk as will form a batter. Beat the whole very hard, then stir the whites of the eggs gently into the mixture. Grease your waffle-irons and bake them. If the batter should be too thin, add a little more flour.

BUTTERMILK CAKES.

358. Take one pint of buttermilk and stir into it as much flour as will form a dough, with one

table spoonful of dissolved carbonate of ammonia. Roll the dough out in sheets, cut the cakes, and bake them in a moderate oven. The carbonate of ammonia may be obtained at any of the druggists; it is the common smelling-salts, without any of the aromatic drugs. It never imparts any taste to the food, as the heat disengages the carbonic acid gas and the ammonia.

INDIAN METLAND.

359. One pint of milk,
    The yelk of one egg and whites of two,
    Half an ounce of butter,
    Salt to the taste,
    Indian meal enough to make a batter.

Warm the milk and butter together, beat the yelk of the egg, stir it into the milk, then add the meal. Lastly whisk the whites till they are very dry, and stir them in gently. Butter a square pan, pour in the batter, and bake in a moderate oven. When done cut it in squares and serve hot.

CREAM OF TARTAR CAKES.

360. One pint of milk,
    One ounce of butter,
    Three pints of flour,
    Three tea spoonsful of cream of tartar,

One tea spoonful of carbonate of soda or salæratus.

Rub the butter in the flour, add the cream of tartar; dissolve the salæratus in the milk and add it to the flour. Roll out the dough, cut it in cakes and bake them on tins in a moderately hot oven.

CAKES.

In the manufacture of cakes it is of very great importance that the materials be of a good quality. It is better to make a plain cake of good materials than a richer one of those of an inferior quality.

Eggs should be beaten in a broad pan until they are *thick*, the yelks when whisked alone will be as thick as batter. The whites when beaten by themselves, should be dry and frothy, and appear full of small white grains. For most cakes the fine white pulverized sugar is best.

The flour should always be sifted, as it renders the cakes lighter.

Never warm butter in the pan it is to be beaten in, as it will be likely to make your cake heavy. If the weather is cold let the butter stand in the warm kitchen some time and it will be soft enough, the action of beating the butter and sugar, and the friction produced, softens the butter sufficiently.

Never beat cakes with your hand, the warmth

of the hand will make them streaked. Always use a wooden ladle for butter and sugar, or batter, and rods or switches for eggs.

FRUIT OR PLUM CAKE, No. 1.

361. One pound of flour,
 One pound of butter,
 One pound of sugar,
 Twelve eggs,
 One pound of citron,
 Two pounds of dried currants, picked and washed,
 One pound of seeded raisins,
 One table spoonful of ground cinnamon,
 Two large nutmegs grated,
 One wine-glass of brandy,
 One wine-glass of wine.

Sift the flour, prepare the spice, wash, pick and dry the currants, and seed the raisins.

With a wooden ladle beat the butter and sugar together in a deep pan. When it is smooth and light, beat the eggs. They should be whisked till they are thick, as the lightness of the cake depends in a great measure upon its being well beaten. Stir in a portion of the egg and flour into the butter and sugar, then a little more, till all is in and thoroughly incorporated. Add the liquor and spice gradually, and lastly the fruit, which must be well floured. Beat the whole fifteen minutes. Butter your pan, line it with two thicknesses of paper well buttered, pour in the batter, and bake about five hours.

Instead of the liquor, rose-water or lemon may be added to suit the taste.

FRUIT OR PLUM CAKE, No. 2.

362. One pound of flour,
   One pound of sugar,
   One pound of butter,
   Ten eggs,
   Two pounds of dried currants, washed, picked and wiped dry,
   Two pounds of raisins, washed, picked and stoned,
   A quarter of a pound of citron, cut in small slices,
   A tea spoonful of ground cinnamon,
   One nutmeg,
   A wine-glass of brandy, and one of wine.

Stir the butter and sugar together till it is very smooth and light. Whisk the eggs till they are as thick as batter, and stir them into the butter and sugar alternately with the flour. Add the spice and liquor very gradually, then the fruit, which must be floured before it is put in, or it will settle at the bottom of the cake and burn. Beat the whole very hard for fifteen minutes.

If it is baked in a tin or iron pan, butter the pan, line the bottom and sides with very thick white or brown paper, butter the paper well, and pour in the mixture. Bake in a moderate oven five hours.

As many object to the use of wine and brandy, this cake may be finely flavored with a glass of rose-water instead; or a little lemon juice and a portion of the rind of the lemon grated in it.

NEW YORK PLUM CAKE.

363.   One pound of butter,
    One pound of sugar,
    One pound of flour,
    One pound of citron, cut in small thin slices,
    Eight eggs,
    Two pounds of raisins, seeded,
    Two pounds of currants,
    A quarter of an ounce of ground cinnamon,
    A quarter of an ounce of ground cloves,
    A quarter of an ounce of ground mace,
    A quarter of an ounce of grated nutmeg,
    One wine-glassful of brandy.

Slice the citron, pick, wash and dry the currants, seed the raisins and mix the fruit together, and dredge over it as much flour as will adhere to it.

Prepare the spice. Stir the butter and sugar till it is smooth and light. Beat the eggs very light and stir them into the butter and sugar. Add the flour and fruit gradually; **beat the batter till the fruit is thoroughly mixed with it, then add slowly the spice and liquor. Beat the mixture very hard for ten or fifteen minutes. Line your pans with two thicknesses of stout white paper, which should be well buttered, pour in the batter, and bake from four to five hours.**

Rose-water and lemon **may be used to flavor it instead of the liquor. A wine-glass of rose-water and as much lemon as to give it a taste.**

POUND CAKE, No. 1.

364. One pound of flour,
One pound of sugar,
One pound and a quarter of butter,
Ten eggs,
One nutmeg grated,
One wine-glass of **rose-water.**

Beat the butter and sugar together; **when it is perfectly light stir in the eggs, which must have been whisked to a thick froth; add the flour, then the nutmeg and rose-water. Beat the whole for a quarter of an hour. Butter your pan, line it with paper, which should be well buttered, and pour in the mixture. Bake it for three hours in a mode-**

rate oven. When the edges of the cake appear to shrink from the sides of the pan the cake will be done.

POUND CAKE, No. 2.

365. One pound of butter,
   One pound of flour,
   One pound of sugar,
   Ten eggs,
   One nutmeg grated,
   One glass of rose-water and brandy mixed.

Beat the butter and sugar to a cream, whisk the eggs till they are very light, then add them to the butter and sugar alternately with the flour. Stir in the spice and liquor, and beat the whole very hard for ten or fifteen minutes. Line your pan with two or three thicknesses of paper well buttered, pour in the mixture, and bake it in a moderate oven for about three hours.

Two pounds of dried currants may be added to this cake if you choose.

COMMON POUND CAKE.

366. One pound of flour,
   One pound of sugar,
   Three-quarters of butter,
   Ten eggs,
   Two tea spoonsful of ground cinnamon,

Two tea spoonsful of grated nutmeg,
A wine-glass of brandy.

Beat the butter and sugar till light and creamy; whisk the eggs till they are thick. Stir the eggs into the butter and sugar, by degrees, alternately with the flour. Add gradually the spice and liquor. Beat the whole very hard for fifteen minutes. Line your pan with paper well buttered; pour in the mixture and bake it in a moderate oven for about three hours. When the edges appear to leave the sides of the pan the cake is nearly done.

This cake is very good, but the spice gives it a dark color. Leave out the spice if you would have your cake a handsome color.

COCOA-NUT POUND CAKE.

367. One pound of butter,
One pound of flour,
One pound of sugar,
One pound of cocoa-nut,
One wine-glass of rose-water,
Ten eggs.

Peel the brown skin off the cocoa-nut and grate it. Beat the butter and sugar to a cream, whisk the eggs and add to it, and stir in the flour. Add gradually the grated nut and rose-water. Beat the mixture very hard for ten or fifteen minutes; butter your pan, line the sides with thick paper, which should be well buttered, pour in the mixture and bake it in a moderate oven for about three hours.

INDIAN POUND CAKE.

368. Three-quarters of a pound of sugar,
Nine ounces of Indian meal,
A quarter of a pound of wheat flour,
Half a pound of butter,
One nutmeg grated,
One tea spoonful of ground cinnamon,
Eight eggs,
Four table spoonsful of brandy.

Mix the wheat and Indian meal together. Stir the butter and sugar to a cream; beat the eggs light and add to it, then the flour; add the spices and liquor; beat it well. Line your pan with paper well buttered and pour in the mixture, or bake it in an earthen mould in a moderate oven.

Rose-water may be substituted for the brandy.

LOAF CAKE.

369. Four cups of flour,
Four cups of sugar,
Two cups of butter,
Six eggs,
Three table spoonsful of brandy,
Two table spoonsful of rose-water,

One grated nutmeg,
One tea spoonful of ground cinnamon,
One cup of milk,
One table spoonful of *dissolved* salæratus.

Beat the butter and sugar to a cream, whisk the eggs very thick, and stir them into the butter and sugar, add the flour, and beat the whole very hard. Add the milk, spice and liquor.

Butter an earthen cake-mould or iron pan, pour in the mixture, and bake about two hours in a moderate oven.

This is a plain cake, and is very good for a lunch.

Instead of the brandy, grated lemon peel may be added.

BRISTOL LOAF CAKE.

370. Five ounces of butter,
Two pounds of flour,
Half a pound of sugar,
One pound of currants,
One table spoonful of powdered cinnamon,
One gill of yeast,
Enough milk to make a thick batter.

Mix the flour, leaving out a quarter of a pound, with the butter cut in small pieces, the sugar, cinnamon and fruit; add milk enough to form a thick batter, and lastly stir in the yeast. Mix it over night and set it away to rise, in the morning stir in the remainder of the flour and let it rise, when light mould it out very lightly, butter your pan, and bake it in an oven about as hot as for bread.

INDIAN LOAF CAKE.

371. One pound of Indian meal,
A quarter of a pound of butter,
Two eggs,
Half a pound of sugar,
A quarter of a pound of raisins,
A quarter of a pound of currants.

Cut up the butter in the Indian meal, pour over it as much boiling milk as will make a thick batter. Beat the eggs very light; when the batter is cool pour them into it. Seed the raisins, wash, pick, and dry the currants, mix them with the raisins, and dredge as much wheat flour on them as will adhere to them. Stir the fruit into the batter and add the sugar. Bake it in a moderate oven two hours.

ALMOND CAKE.

372. Ten eggs,
One pound of sugar,
Half a pound of flour,

One wine-glass of rose-water,
One ounce of bitter almonds.

Beat the eggs, the yelks and whites separate, when the yelks are very light add the sugar and the almonds, which must have been blanched and pounded with the rose-water. Beat the whole well. Whisk the whites to a dry froth, and stir in one-half the white with one-half the flour till it is thoroughly mixed, then add the other half of the white and flour.

Do not beat it after the white is in, as that will make it tough and heavy.

SPONGE CAKE, No. 1.

373. Three-quarters of a pound of flour,
Twelve eggs,
One pound of sugar,
A table spoonful of rose-water.

Beat the yelks and sugar together until they are very light. Whisk the whites till they are perfectly dry, add the rose-water, then the whites and flour alternately, but do not beat it after the whites are in. Butter your pans, or if you wish to bake it in one large cake, grease a mould, pour in the mixture, and bake it. The small cakes should have sugar sifted over them before they are set in the oven, and the oven should be hot.

SPONGE CAKE, No. 2.

374. One pound of sugar,
Three quarters of a pound of flour,
Ten eggs.

Dissolve the sugar in one gill of water, then put it over the fire and let it boil. Beat the eggs a few minutes, till the yelks and whites are thoroughly mixed together, then stir in *very gradually* the boiling sugar; beat the eggs hard all the time you are pouring the sugar on them. Beat the mixture for three-quarters of an hour; it will get very light. Stir in the flour very gently, and add the grated rind of a lemon. Butter your pan and set it in the oven immediately.

SPONGE CAKE, No. 3.

375. Five eggs,
Half a pound of loaf sugar,
The grated rind and juice of one lemon,
A quarter of a pound of flour.

Separate the yelks from the whites. Beat the yelks and sugar together until they are very light, then add the whites after they have been whisked to a dry froth, alternately with the flour. Stir in the lemon, put the mixture in small pans, sift sugar over them, and bake them.

JUMBLES.

376.   One pound of sugar,
   Three-quarters of a pound of butter,
   One pound of flour,
   Five eggs,
   One table spoonful of rose-water.

Beat the butter and sugar till smooth and light. Whisk the eggs, stir them into the butter and sugar, then add the rose-water and flour. Roll the dough in strips half an inch wide and four inches long, join them at both ends so as to form rings, sift sugar over, place them on tins, and bake them in a slow oven.

SPANISH JUMBLES.

377.   One pound of butter,
   One pound of sugar,
   Eight eggs,
   Flour sufficient to form a soft dough,
   One nutmeg,
   One tea spoonful of ground cinnamon.

Beat the butter and sugar to a cream. Whisk the eggs very light and add them to it with the spice, and stir in flour enough to form a soft dough.

Roll the dough in strips about four inches long, join the ends so as to form rings. Butter your tins or pans, place them on them, but do not let them touch each other, and bake in a rather quick oven.

PLAIN JUMBLES.

378. Two pounds of flour,
One pound and a quarter of sugar,
Half a pint of milk,
Three eggs, and a half pound of butter,
One tea spoonful of *dissolved* salæratus,
Essence of lemon to the taste.

Beat the butter and sugar to a cream; add the eggs, which must have been whisked till very thick, and some essence of lemon, then pour in the milk and salæratus. The salæratus should be dissolved in water, and a tea spoonful of this solution be mixed with the milk.

Bake in the form of jumbles.

COCOA-NUT JUMBLES.

379. Half a pound of butter,
One pound of grated cocoa-nut,
Three eggs,
One pound of white sugar,
One table spoonful of rose-water,
As much flour as will form a dough.

Peel off the brown skin, wash the cocoa-nut and grate it. Beat the butter and sugar to a cream.

Whisk the eggs and add to it, with the rose-water and grated nut. Lastly stir in the flour; as much as will form a dough. Roll it out in strips about four inches long, join the ends and bake them on buttered tins.

GINGER FRUIT CAKE.

380. Three-quarters of a pound of sugar,
Three-quarters of a pound of butter,
Two pounds of flour,
Six eggs,
One quart of molasses,
One pound of raisins,
Half a pound of currants,
Two table spoonsful of ginger,
One table spoonful of salæratus,
Two table spoonsful of cinnamon.

Beat the butter and sugar to a cream. Add to this the eggs well beaten, then the ginger and cinnamon, and molasses and flour. Stir all very hard. Flour the fruit and stir in last, with the salæratus.

Line your pan with several thicknesses of buttered paper, pour in the mixture, and bake in a slow oven.

GINGER CUP CAKE.

381. Two cups of butter,
Two cups of sugar,

One cup of molasses,
One cup of cream,
Three eggs,
One table spoonful of dissolved salæratus,
Four heaping cups of flour,
Half a cup of ginger.

Beat the butter and sugar **to a cream. Whisk the eggs light and add to it, then stir in the other ingredients.** Butter a pan or earthen **mould and pour in the mixture, bake in a moderate oven. Or it may** be baked in queen-cake pans.

GINGER-NUTS.

382. **Half a pound of butter,**
   Half a pound of sugar,
   One pint of molasses,
   Two ounces of ginger,
   Half an ounce of ground cloves and allspice mixed,
   Two table spoonsful of cinnamon,
   As much flour as will form a **dough.**

Stir the butter and sugar together; add the spice, ginger, molasses, and flour enough to form a dough. Knead it well, make it out in small cakes, bake them on tins in a very moderate oven. Wash them over with molasses and water before they are put in to bake.

GINGER-BREAD, No. 1.

383. One pound of sugar,
One pound of butter,
Three pounds of flour,
Two table spoonsful of ginger,
One gill of cream,
One pint of molasses.

Rub the butter in the flour; add the other ingredients. Roll out the dough, cut it into cakes, place them on buttered tins, and bake in a moderately cool oven.

Wash the cakes over with molasses and water before you bake them.

GINGER-BREAD, No. 2.

384. Half a pound of sugar, *[1 cup]*
Half a pound of butter, *[½ cup]*
One pound and a half of flour,
One ounce of ginger, *[2 tablespoonful]*
One pint of molasses. *[2 kitchen cups]*

Rub the flour and butter well together, add the other ingredients. Roll out the dough, cut it in cakes, place them on tins, wash ~~them~~ over with molasses and water and bake ~~them~~ in a very moderate oven.

BOSTON GINGER-BREAD.

385. Three cups of flour,

One cup of butter,
One cup of molasses,
Two eggs,
One table spoonful of *dissolved* salæratus,
Two large table spoonsful of ginger,
One table spoonful of cinnamon,
Milk enough to form a dough,

Rub the butter and flour together, and add the other ingredients. Roll it out in sheets, cut them, butter your tins, place them, and wash the cakes over with molasses and water before they are put in the oven. They require a very moderate heat to bake them, as they easily scorch.

COMMON GINGER-BREAD.

386. Half a pound of butter,
Half a tea cupful of ginger,
One pint of molasses,
Two pounds of flour,
One table spoonful of salæratus.

Rub the flour and butter together and add the other ingredients. Knead the dough well. Roll it out, cut it in cakes, wash them over with molasses and water, and bake them in a moderate oven.

PLAIN GINGER-BREAD.

387. Three pounds of flour,

A quarter of a pound of sugar,
Half an ounce of ground ginger,
Half a pound of butter,
Molasses sufficient to moisten the flour.

Cut up the butter in the flour, add to it the sugar and ginger, and stir in molasses barely enough to moisten the flour, as it will become softer by kneading. Knead the dough well, roll it out in sheets, cut it in cakes, place them on tins, wash them over with molasses and water, and bake in a cool oven.

SODA BISCUIT.

388. Six ounces of butter,
Six ounces of sugar,
One tea spoonful of the carbonate of soda,
One pint of milk,
Flour enough to form a dough.

Melt the butter in the milk and dissolve the soda in it. Stir in the sugar, and add flour enough to form a stiff dough.

Knead it well, roll it out thin, then knead it up again until it is smooth and light. Roll it out in sheets about a quarter of an inch thick, cut it into cakes, and bake them in a rather hot oven.

KISSES, OR CREAM CAKE.

389. The whites of three eggs,

One drop of essence of lemon,
As much powdered sugar as will thicken the eggs.

—

Whisk the whites to a dry froth, then add the powdered sugar, a tea spoonful at a time, till the egg is as thick as very thick batter.

Wet a sheet of white paper, place it on a tin, and drop the egg and sugar on it in lumps about the shape and size of a walnut.

Set them in a cool oven, and as soon as the surface is hardened take them out; with a broad bladed knife, take them off the paper, place the flat parts of two together, put them on a sieve in a very cool oven to dry.

SUGAR CAKE.

390. Half a pound of butter,
 Half a pound of sugar,
 One pound of flour,
 Three eggs,
 Milk enough to form a dough.

—

Beat the butter and sugar together. Whisk the eggs light and add them, then stir in the milk and flour alternately, so as to form a dough.

Roll it out, cut it in cakes, and bake them in a moderate oven.

FEDERAL CAKE.

391. Two pounds of flour,
One pound of sugar,
Three-quarters of a pound of butter,
Four eggs,
The juice of one lemon,
One table spoonful of dissolved salæratus,
Two tea spoonsful of cinnamon,
Milk enough to form a dough.

Rub the butter and flour together, add the sugar and beaten egg, then the salæratus, lemon, cinnamon, and milk. Roll out the dough in sheets, cut the cakes in the form of a diamond, and bake in a tolerably hot oven.

WHITE CUP CAKE.

392. One cup of butter,
Two cups of sugar,
Three cups of flour,
The whites of eight eggs,
A small table spoonful of salæratus,
A table spoonful of rose-water,
Milk or cream to make a thick batter.

Beat the butter and sugar to a cream. Whisk the eggs very light, and add them gradually with the flour, add the rose-water and salæratus, and if this should not be quite as thin as pound cake batter, add a little rich milk or cream. Fill small tins about three parts full with the mixture and bake them.

The yelks of the eggs which are left may be used for a pudding.

GERMAN CAKE.

393. Three-quarters of a pound of butter,
One pound and a half of sugar,
Four eggs
Two pounds of flour,
One tea spoonful of nutmeg,
Half a wine glass of rose-water,
One pound of dried currants.

Beat the butter and sugar together. Whisk the eggs, and add with the other ingredients. Roll out the dough in sheets, cut them in cakes with a tin cutter or the top of a tumbler. Bake in a moderate oven.

SEED CAKE.

394. Half a pound of butter,
Three tea cups of sugar,
One pound of flour,
One tea spoonful of carraway seed,
Half a table spoonful of salæratus,
As much milk as will form a dough.

Rub the butter in the flour and sugar, then add the seed, salæratus, and milk.

Knead the dough till it is smooth. Roll it out, cut it in cakes, and bake them in a moderately hot oven.

CURRANT CAKE.

395. A quarter of a pound of butter,
Half a pound of flour,
Two ounces of currants,
Six ounces of sugar,
Two eggs,
A table spoonful of brandy or rose-water,
Milk enough to form a dough.

Rub the butter, sugar, and flour together with the fruit, which must have been washed, picked, and dried. Beat the eggs and add with the brandy or rose-water, and milk enough to form a dough. Roll it out thin, cut it into cakes.

ROCK CAKE.

396. Three eggs, (the whites only.)
Three-quarters of a pound of sugar,
Three-quarters of a pound of sweet and bitter almonds.

Whisk the eggs very light and dry, then add gradually a tea spoonful of the sugar at a time.

Beat it hard until all the sugar is in. Blanch the almonds, cut them in pieces about the size of a pea, mix them with the egg, drop them on sheets of white paper, and bake them in a cool oven.

ELECTION CAKE.

397. Two pounds of sugar,
  Three quarters of a pound of butter,
  One pint of milk made into a sponge,
  Four eggs,
  Two table spoonsful of cinnamon,
  And flour enough to make a dough.

Set a sponge the evening before with a pint of milk, a gill of yeast, a little salt, and flour enough to make a thick batter. The next morning stir the butter and sugar together, whisk the eggs, and add to it with the sponge and other ingredients, and flour enough to form a dough. Knead it, butter your pan, put in the dough; let it rise. When it is light bake it.

DEVONSHIRE CAKES.

398. Half a pound of sugar,
  A quarter of a pound of butter,
  Four eggs,
  One tea spoonful of grated nutmeg,

One ounce of carraway seed,
And flour enough to form a dough.

Beat the eggs very light, stir the butter and sugar to a cream, and mix them together, with the nutmeg, carraway seed and flour. Knead the dough, roll it out rather thin, cut the cakes, butter your tins, put them on so as not to touch each other.

SCOTCH CAKE.

399. Three-quarters of a pound of butter,
One pound of sugar,
One pound of flour,
One gill of milk,
One large table spoonful of powdered cinnamon.

Stir the butter and sugar together, then add the cinnamon, flour and milk; roll out the dough into sheets, cut it in cakes and bake them in a moderate oven until they are brown.

CRULLERS.

400. Five eggs,
Three-quarters of a pound of sugar,
A quarter of a pound of butter,
One table spoonful of ground cinnamon,
Two table spoonsful of brandy,

One table spoonful of salæratus,
As much flour as will form a soft dough.

—

Beat the butter and sugar together till it is light. Whisk the eggs, and then stir in the spice and liquor. Beat the whole very hard; add the salæratus, and as much flour as will form a soft dough, cut it in strips, twist them and drop them in a pot of boiling lard. When they are of a light brown they will be done. Sift sugar over them when cold.

—

DUTCH LOAF.

401. A quarter of a pound of butter,
Half a pound of sugar,
One pound of dried currants,
Two table spoonsful of cinnamon,
A pint of sponge,
As much flour as will form a dough.

—

Make a sponge the evening before you wish to bake the cake, of a tea cupful and a half of milk, and as much flour stirred into it as will form a *thick* batter, with a little salt, and one gill of good yeast. In the morning this sponge should be light. Then beat the butter and sugar together, add the cinnamon, currants and sponge, with flour enough to form a dough. Butter a pan, and when it is light, bake it in an oven about as hot as for bread.

RICE CUP CAKE.

402. Two cups of sugar,
Two cups of butter,
One cup and a half of rice flour,
Half a cup of wheat flour,
Ten eggs,
A tea spoonful of nutmeg,
Half a pound of currants,
Half a gill of rose-water.

Beat the butter and sugar very light; whisk the eggs till they are very thick, and stir in; add the nutmeg and the flour gradually, then the rose-water. Beat the whole very hard for ten minutes. Stir in the fruit, which must be floured to prevent it from sinking to the bottom of the cake.

Butter a pan, line it with thick paper well buttered, and bake it in a moderate oven. Or you may bake the batter in small pans.

COCOA-NUT CAKES.

403. Three eggs,
Ten ounces of sugar,
As much grated cocoa-nut as will form a stiff paste.

Whisk the eggs very light and dry, add the sugar gradually, and when all the sugar is in stir in the cocoa-nut. Roll a table spoonful of the mixture in your hands in the form of a pyramid, place them on paper, put the paper on tins, and bake in a rather cool oven till they are just a little brown.

SPANISH BUNS.

404. One pound of flour,
   Three-quarters of a pound of sugar,
   Half a pound of butter,
   Two table spoonsful of rose-water,
   Four eggs,
   One gill of yeast,
   One tea spoonful of cinnamon,
   Half a tea spoonful of nutmeg,
   Half a pint of milk.

Cut up the butter and rub it well with the flour, add the sugar, beat the eggs very light, and stir in lastly the spices and rose-water, with milk enough to form a very thick batter, then add the yeast. The next morning stir it again and let it rise the second time. Butter your pans and fill them three parts full. When they are done and cold sift sugar over, and with a sharp knife cut them in squares.

BUNS.

405. One pound of flour,
   Three ounces of butter,

A quarter of a pound of sugar,
Two eggs,
Three half gills of milk,
One gill of home-made yeast,
One table spoonful of rose-water,
Two tea spoonsful of powdered cinnamon.

Warm the butter in the milk. Beat the eggs. Mix the eggs with the milk and butter, and pour altogether into the pan of flour, then add the rose-water, cinnamon and yeast. Mix all thoroughly, knead the dough well, let it rise, when light make it out into cakes, put them in buttered pans, let them stand till they rise again and bake them.

DOUGH-NUTS.

406. Three pounds of flour,
A quarter of a pound of butter,
One pound of sugar, four eggs,
One gill of yeast,
One tea spoonful of cinnamon,
One nutmeg grated,
One table spoonful of rose-water,
Milk enough to form a soft dough.

Rub the butter and flour well together, and add the spices and sugar. Whisk the eggs, stir them in with the rose-water and yeast, and milk enough to form a soft dough. Stand it away to rise;

when light roll it out very lightly, cut it in diamonds, or any shape you choose, and drop them into a pot of boiling lard. Sift sugar over when *&c.*

MACAROONS.

408. Three eggs,
Three-quarters of a pound of powdered white sugar,
Half a pound of sweet almonds,
Two ounces of bitter almonds.

Whisk the eggs till they are very dry, then add gradually a tea spoonful of the sugar at a time, for if too much is put in at once it will thin the egg. Beat it hard until all the sugar is in. Have your almonds blanched and bruised in a mortar, but they must not be pounded to a paste. Then stir in the almonds, drop a spoonful in a place, on sheets of white paper laid on tins, and bake them in a cool oven till they have just a tinge of brown.

LADY CAKE.

408. Three-quarters of a pound of butter,
Three-quarters of a pound of sugar,
One pound of flour,
The whites of sixteen eggs,

Half an ounce of bitter almonds,
Two table spoonsful of rose water.

Beat the butter and sugar to a cream; pour boiling water over the almonds, let them stand a little time, blanch them, pound them in a mortar, adding but a few at a time, with a little rose-water to prevent them from getting oily, add to them the remainder of the rose-water, then stir the almonds into the butter and sugar. Whisk the whites very dry, and stir them gradually into the butter and sugar with the flour. Butter your pans and bake them in a moderate oven. It may be baked in one large cake.

COMPOSITION CAKE.

409. Two cups of butter,
Three cups of sugar,
Five cups of flour,
Five eggs,
One cup of milk,
One tea spoonful of dissolved salæratus,
Two table spoonsful of brandy,
One pound of raisins,
Half a nutmeg grated.

Stir the butter and sugar to a cream, beat the eggs and add to it, then the spice, liquor and salæratus; lastly the raisins, which must be seeded and floured. Line your pans with paper well buttered, pour in the mixture, and bake in a moderate oven.

SCOTCH LOAF.

410. One pound of flour,
Three-quarters of a pound of butter,
Three-quarters of a pound of sugar,
Ten eggs,
Half a gill of rose-water,
One table spoonful of *dissolved* salæratus,
One pound of dried currants,
Two tea spoonsful of ground cinnamon.

Pick, wash and dry the currants, and dredge as much flour over as will adhere to them. Beat the butter and sugar till it is smooth and light; whisk the eggs to a froth, stir them into the butter and sugar alternately with the flour; add the spice and liquor, beat the whole very hard for ten minutes; lastly stir in the fruit and salæratus. Butter an earthen cake mould or iron pan, pour in the mixture, and bake for about two hours in a moderate oven.

FRENCH CAKE.

411. One pound of sugar,
Three-quarters of a pound of butter,
One pound and a half of flour,

Twelve eggs,
Half a wine glass of wine,
Half a wine glass of brandy,
Half a tea cupful of milk,
Half a grated nutmeg,
A quarter of a pound of seeded raisins,
A quarter of a pound of citron,
Half a pound of currants,
A quarter of a pound of sweet almonds.

—

Seed the raisins, slice the citron in very small thin pieces, wash, pick, and dry the currants, prepare the spice, pour some hot water on the almonds, let them stand a few minutes, then take each kernel between the thumb and finger, gently press it and the skin will come off. Put them in a marble or wedgewood mortar, and pound them to a paste; add a little water or milk to them whilst you are pounding them, or they will be oily.

Mix your fruit together, and dredge as much flour over it as will adhere to it.

Beat the butter and sugar together till it is perfectly light and smooth. Whisk the yelks of the eggs, without the whites, till they are very thick. Stir the yelks into the butter and sugar. Add to this the spice, liquor, and almonds. Beat it very hard for five minutes. Whisk the whites till they are dry and present a grained appearance.

Stir the whites and flour into the batter alternately, but do not beat it after the whites are in; just stir it sufficiently to mix the flour thoroughly. Lastly stir in the fruit.

Line your pans with thick paper well buttered, and pour in the mixture. Bake in a moderate oven for three hours.

A wine glassful of rose-water may be used instead of the wine and brandy.

TRAVELER'S BISCUIT.

412. Two pounds of flour,
　Three-quarters of a pound of sugar,
　A quarter of a pound of butter,
　One tea spoonful of *dissolved* salæratus,
　Milk sufficient to form a dough.

Cut up the butter in the flour, add the sugar, and put in the salæratus and milk together, so as to form a dough.

Knead it till it becomes perfectly smooth and light. Roll it in sheets about the eighth of an inch thick, cut the cakes with a cutter or the top of a tumbler. Bake in a moderate oven.

LIGHT SUGAR BISCUITS.

413. One pound and a half of powdered white sugar,
　Half a pint of milk made into a sponge,

Two ounces of butter,
As much flour as will form a dough,
One gill of yeast.

Make a sponge with the half pint of milk and as much flour stirred into it as will form a thick batter, add the yeast and a little salt. This should be done in the evening. The next morning cut the butter in small pieces, place it near the fire where it will dissolve, but not get hot, add this to the sponge, with as much flour as will form a dough. Stand it to rise, and when light, butter your tins, make out the dough in biscuits, but take care not to handle it more that you can help, put the cakes on tins, and when they are light bake them in a very hot oven. When they are done wash them over with a brush dipped in sugar dissolved in water and sift sugar over the top.

PLAIN CUP CAKE.

414. One cup of butter,
Two cups of sugar,
Two cups of flour,
Four eggs,
Half a grated nutmeg,
Table spoonful of rose-water.

Stir the butter and sugar together till very light Whisk the eggs till they are thick, and stir them into the butter and sugar alternately with the flour. Add the nutmeg and rose-water. Beat the whole very hard. Butter some cups or shallow pans, pour in the mixture, and bake in a moderate oven.

APEES.

415. Three-quarters of a pound of flour,
  Half a pound of butter,
  Half a pound of sugar,
  One tea spoonful of grated nutmeg,
  As much milk as will form a dough.

Cut up the butter in the flour, add the sugar, and spice by degrees.

Stir in as much milk as will make a dough. Knead it well, roll it out in sheets, cut it in cakes, Butter your tins, lay them on so as not to touch, and bake in a moderate oven.

SHREWSBURY CAKE.

416. One pound of flour,
  Three-quarters of a pound of sugar,
  Half a pound of butter,
  Five eggs,
  Half a nutmeg.

Beat the butter and sugar together. Whisk the

eggs and add to it, with the nutmeg. Stir in the flour, roll out the dough and cut it in cakes. Bake in a quick oven.

DOVER BISCUITS.

417. Half a pound of butter,
Half a pound of sugar,
Three-quarters of a pound of flour,
Two eggs,
One table spoonful of rose-water,
Half a tea spoonful of nutmeg.

Stir the butter and sugar together. Beat the eggs light and stir into it, with the rose-water; add the spice and flour. Roll out thin and cut into small cakes.

WASHINGTON CAKE, No. 1.

418. One pound of butter,
One pound of flour,
One pound of sugar,
Six eggs,
One wine glass of wine,
One wine glass of brandy,
One grated nutmeg,
One table spoonful of cinnamon,
Two pounds of dried currants,
One table spoonful of *dissolved* salæratus,
Half a pint of rich milk.

Stir the butter and sugar to a cream. Beat the eggs very light and stir into it, then add the liquor, spice, and milk, then stir in the flour, lastly the salæratus and fruit.

Butter a pan and bake it.

WASHINGTON CAKE, No. 2.

419. One pound of sugar,
Three-quarters of a pound of butter,
Four eggs,
One pound of flour,
One tea cupful of milk,
Two tea spoonsful of *dissolved* salæratus,
Three table spoonsful of brandy,
Half a tea spoonful of cinnamon,
Half a nutmeg,
One pound of dried currants washed, picked, and wiped dry.

Beat the butter and sugar until it is smooth and light. Whisk the eggs till they are thick and add them to the butter and sugar. Stir in the flour, brandy, and spice. Flour the fruit and stir it in. Beat the whole very hard for fifteen minutes. Then stir in the salæratus.

Line the sides and bottom of your pan with thick paper, butter it well, pour in the mixture and bake it in a moderate oven.

For those who object to the use of brandy, two table spoonsful of rose-water may be substituted in its place.

SUGAR BISCUITS.

420. Three-quarters of a pound of sugar,
Half a pound of butter,
One pint of milk,
One tea spoonful of carbonate of soda,
Flour sufficient to make a dough.

Melt the sugar, butter, and soda in the milk.

When the milk is lukewarm stir in the flour till it forms a dough. Knead it well for a very long time, then roll it out in sheets, and with a sharp knife cut it in squares, butter your tins, and bake them in a hot oven.

PRESERVES.

Fruit for preserving should be carefully selected, it should never be bruised, and always be of the largest kind and fairest quality.

No sugar will make handsome preserves but the purest white. It may be pulverized or in the loaf. Besides, it is a mistaken idea that low priced sugars are cheaper for preserves, for they must be boiled much longer in order to collect the great amount of scum which arises on the syrup, consequently the evaporation reduces the quantity.

Very little white of egg or isinglass is sufficient to clarify an ordinary sized kettle of syrup. If too much of either is used it froths on the surface and is of no utility.

Preserves should always be boiled smartly; many persons would be more successful with their preserving if they would let their fruit boil fast. When permitted to simmer it breaks in pieces.

All jellies and preserves should be put in the jars while lukewarm, as the jelly or syrup, if it be thick, breaks after it has become cold; the jars should be left open till the next day.

Glass jars of a small size, or large tumblers, are better for preserves than china, for should they not keep well it can be detected immediately.

Each jar should have a piece of white paper cut the size of the top, dip the paper in brandy or spirits of wine and lay it on the preserves; then cut another piece about a quarter of an inch larger than the mouth of the jar; cut the edge of it in slits nearly a quarter of an inch long; cover this edge with paste, place the paper over the jar and lap the edge over on the side of the jar, which may easily be done, as the strips will lap one over the other.

Each jar should have the name of the contents written on the cover.

Preserves should be kept in a cool dry place.

CALF'S FOOT JELLY.

421. To one set of feet pour three quarts of water. Let it boil till reduced to one half, then strain the liquor through a jelly bag and stand it away to get cold. When it is cold scrape off the cake of fat, and in order to cleanse the jelly from all the grease wipe the surface with a damp sponge, also the sides of the vessel which contains it. Cut up the jelly and put it in your preserving kettle, but be careful not to take the sediment which settles at the bottom. To each pint of this jelly add half a pound of the very best white sugar, and a quarter of an ounce of Russian isinglass dissolved in warm water, one tea cupful of Madeira wine, and the juice and rind of two lemons. When the sugar is dissolved set the kettle over the fire and boil it for twenty minutes. Then pour it into your jelly bag and let it drip but do not squeeze the bag. As soon as it has all dripped through turn the bag, scrape it well but do not wash it, and, strain your jelly again. Repeat this till it is perfectly clear. Pour it in the moulds while it is warm and let them stand open till the jelly is cold. When you wish to turn it out of the moulds wring a napkin out of hot water and wrap it round the moulds for a minute or two, then turn the moulds upside down, and the jelly will turn out.

FOX GRAPE JELLY.

422. Take green fox grapes, wash them and

put them in a preserving kettle with just water enough to pulp them. When they are tender mash and strain them through a sieve, to free them from the seeds and skin. To each pint of the pulp add a pound of the best white sugar, and a piece of isinglass about an inch square, dissolved in warm water. When the sugar has dissolved stir it well, and place the kettle over the fire. Let it boil fifteen or twenty minutes, then try it by dropping a little in a glass of cold water, if it falls to the bottom without mixing with the water the jelly is done. Pass it through a jelly bag, pour it into your glasses while warm, and let it stand till the next day before the glasses are pasted.

CRANBERRY JELLY, No. 1.

423. Pick and wash your cranberries, which should be very ripe, and put them over the fire with half a pint of water to each quart of cranberries. Stew them till they are soft, then mash them and strain the juice through a jelly bag; to each pint of juice add one pound of loaf or pulverized white sugar, with some isinglass, in the proportion of half an ounce to two quarts of juice. Dissolve the isinglass in as much warm water as will cover it; when perfectly dissolved, which will require a couple of hours, pour it in with the sugar and juice. When the sugar is dissolved set the kettle over the

fire, and boil and skim it till a jelly is formed, which you can tell by dropping a little in a glass of cold water. If it falls to the bottom without mingling with the water the jelly is done. When it is lukewarm pour it in glasses and let them stand till the following day, then cover them with brandy paper and paste them closely.

CRANBERRY JELLY, No. 2.

424. Dissolve one ounce of Russian isinglass in three half-pints of warm water. Strain it through your flannel jelly-bag. Add to this three pints of cranberry juice with four pounds of sugar; boil and skim it. As soon as the scum has ceased to rise strain it and put it in moulds. The sugar should be of the best quality.

ORANGE JELLY.

425. Squeeze the juice from the oranges, and to every pint of the juice add a pound of sugar and a quarter of an ounce of dissolved isinglass. The Russian isinglass is the kind to use for this purpose. Boil and skim it till a jelly is formed, which you may tell by letting a drop fall in a glass of cold water, and if it falls to the bottom in a mass the jelly is done. Or, take a little out in a spoon and expose it to the cool air for a few minutes.

STRAWBERRY JELLY.

426. Stem the strawberries, put them in a pan, and with a wooden spoon or potato masher rub them fine. Put a sieve over a pan, and inside of the sieve spread a piece of thin muslin; strain the juice through this, and to a pint add one pound of sugar, with a quarter of an ounce of isinglass dissolved in water to every five pounds of sugar. When the sugar is dissolved set the kettle over the fire and boil it till it is to a jelly. Pour it into glasses while it is warm, and paste them when cold.

CURRANT JELLY.

427. Mash your fruit with a wooden spoon, and squeeze the juice through your jelly bag. To every pint of juice allow a pound of white sugar. When the sugar is dissolved, add a piece of isinglass dissolved in warm water to clarify the jelly. A quarter of an ounce of isinglass to five pints of juice will be sufficient. Boil and skim it till a jelly is formed; then take it off the fire and put it in glasses while warm. The next day put brandy paper over them and paste them.

Black currant jelly is made in the same way, only it requires but three-quarters of a pound of sugar to a pint of juice.

QUINCE JELLY.

428. Pare and core your quinces, and as you pare them throw them into cold water. Put them into a preserving kettle with water enough to cover them, and let them boil till the fruit is tender. Then put a sieve over a pan, pour the fruit and water into it and let it drain, but do not mash the fruit; strain the juice through the jelly bag. To each pint of juice thus obtained add one pound of loaf or pulverized white sugar; and to every five pounds of sugar add a quarter of an ounce of isinglass dissolved in hot water. When the sugar is dissolved put it over the fire and boil and skim it till a jelly is formed, which you can discover by dropping a little in a glass of cold water; if it sinks to the bottom without mingling with the water the jelly is done. Pour it in your glasses when it is lukewarm, and let them stand open till it is entirely cold. Cover with brandy paper, and paste paper over the top.

If you wish to have *light colored* jelly, never put in the parings, as they always make it dark. A jelly may be made of the parings and cores for family use.

Apple jelly may be made in the same manner as the quince. The pulp of the apple, which is left after the jelly is made, may be sweetened for pies. The pulp of the quince may be made into marmalade according to the following receipt:

QUINCE MARMALADE.

429. To each pound of the pulp obtained according to the above receipt for jelly, add one pound of white sugar; boil the whole until it is perfectly smooth. It must be stirred all the time it is boiling. If you do not make jelly of your quinces cut them up in small pieces, add a pound of sugar to a pound of fruit, and as much water as will dissolve the sugar; then boil it till it is a perfectly smooth paste; stir it all the time.

PEACH MARMALADE.

430. Pare and cut up the peaches in small pieces, and to a pound of fruit add a pound of sugar. When the sugar is dissolved set it over the fire and let it boil till it is a smooth paste. Stir it all the time it is boiling. Put it in the jars while warm and paste them over the next day.

PRESERVED PEARS.

431. Peel the pears, and if they are large, cut each one in four pieces, and take out the core.

To a pound of fruit weigh a pound of sugar; dissolve the sugar with just enough water to wet it, add a quarter of an ounce of isinglass dissolved in warm water to five pounds of sugar. When the sugar is dissolved, make the syrup as directed for preserved peaches, and cook the fruit in the same manner.

PRESERVED QUINCES.

432. Pare and core the fruit, cut them in quarters, and boil them in water untill tender. Weigh the fruit and add a pound of sugar to each pound of fruit. Put the sugar in a preserving-kettle with two wine-glasses of water to each pound of sugar, and a quarter of an ounce of isinglass dissolved in warm water to every six pounds of fruit. When the sugar is dissolved set it over the fire, boil and skim it till no more scum rises. Then pour the syrup in another vessel, wash the kettle so as to free it from any scum which may adhere to it, pour the jelly back in the kettle and put in the fruit. Set it over a brisk fire and let it boil for about an hour and a half, or until the fruit looks clear when held towards the light. It should always boil hard or the preserves will be dark colored. When it appears translucent take it off the fire; take the fruit out a piece at a time, and lay it on broad dishes. Strain the syrup, and when it is lukewarm put the fruit in your jars and pour the syrup over. When cold cover with brandy paper and paste them closely.

PRESERVED PINE-APPLE.

433. Scald the slices in water till tender; then

make a syrup of a pound of sugar to a pound of fruit, and proceed as directed for quinces.

PRESERVED PEACHES.

434. Choose the white cling-stones, known by the name of the "Heath peach." Insert the knife at the stem and cut them longitudinally through to the stone. Wring out the stones by placing one hand on each half of the peach and suddenly give each a turn in opposite directions; the fruit will break in half, leaving the stone attached to one side. With a pointed knife it may easily be extracted. After the peaches have all been prepared in this manner pare and weigh them. Then weigh a pound of sugar for each pound of fruit. Put the sugar into a preserving kettle, and allow a gill of water to each pound of sugar. Let the sugar stand until it is perfectly dissolved before it is put on the fire; to ten pounds of sugar add the half of the white of an egg, well beaten, or a piece of Russian isinglass, about an inch square, dissolved in two table spoonsful of water. Set the kettle over the fire, and as soon as the syrup begins to boil skim it. When the scum has ceased to rise, take the syrup off the fire, pour it into a pan, and wash the kettle in order to prevent the scum which adheres to the sides from boiling into the fruit. Now pour the syrup back into the kettle, add the fruit to it, and place it over a brisk fire, let the fruit boil fast

for about an hour and a quarter, or until it appears translucent when held on a fork towards the light. Then take your peaches out very carefully, a piece at a time; place them on dishes so as merely to touch. Pour the syrup in pans, and let it stand until it is about lukewarm. Then put the fruit into your jars and pour the syrup over; paste the jars the next day.

PRESERVED FRESH FIGS.

435. Select the fruit when fully ripe, though not soft, pick them carefully that they may not be broken. Pour boiling water over them, and let them simmer for five minutes.

Preserve them as other fruits.

PRESERVED CITRON MELON.

436. Cut off the hard rind of the melon (which should be the *preserving* citron, not the green cantelope) and cut it in pieces of any size and shape you choose: the slices should be from a quarter to half an inch thick. Weigh your fruit, and to every pound add one of sugar. Put the sugar in a preserving kettle with a gill of water to each pound of sugar and some isinglass dissolved in warm water; it will require a quarter of an ounce of isinglass to every five pounds of fruit. When the sugar is dissolved, put it over the fire and boil and

skim it. Then pour the syrup out of the kettle, wash it and return the syrup to it. Now put in the fruit, and set it over a brisk fire, where it will boil rapidly. When the fruit appears translucent when held up towards the light it is done. It will take from an hour and a quarter to an hour and a half to cook it.

Then take it out a piece at a time, spread it on dishes, and strain the syrup in a pan. When the syrup is lukewarm, put your fruit in the jars and pour it over. Let them stand till next day, put brandy paper over and paste them.

This fruit may be flavored with lemons sliced and preserved with it. Do not peel the lemons, cut them in thin slices, and cook them with the fruit. To three pounds of fruit add one lemon. As the citron makes a beautiful but tasteless preserve, it is necessary to flavor it with lemon, orange, or some other fruit. If, when it is a little cool, it should not taste sufficiently of the lemon, a few drops of the essence of lemon may be added.

PRESERVED GREEN GAGES.

437. Prepare the fruit by pricking each one with a needle to prevent them from bursting.

Leave a portion of the stem on each, as it gives small fruits a handsome appearance on the table. Make a syrup of a pound of sugar to each pound of fruit; and a gill of water to a pound of sugar.

Add a quarter of an ounce of isinglass, dissolved in warm water, to every six pounds of sugar. When the sugar is dissolved put it with the dissolved isinglass over the fire, boil and skim it. Then pour it out of the kettle, wash the kettle, put the syrup back again, put in the fruit, and boil it till by holding one towards the light it looks clear. Take the gages out one at a time, strain the syrup; put the fruit in jars, and pour the syrup over warm. Paste them up the next day.

PRESERVED PLUMS.

438. These are preserved in the same manner as gages, only they are skinned by pouring hot water over them; the skins will peel off nicely and leave the stems attached to the fruit.

STRAWBERRY JAM.

439. Put together equal weights of fruit and sugar, mash all well, put it into a preserving kettle, and boil it about twenty minutes. While it is warm put it in jars, and paste it when cold.

CHERRY JAM.

440. This is better when made of fine morella cherries. Wash the cherries and put them on to stew with a gill of water to a pound of fruit. When perfectly tender, pass them through a colander to

extract the stones. To a pound of the pulp add a pound of sugar, when the sugar is dissolved put it over the fire, and boil it to a smooth paste.

RASPBERRY JAM.

441. To a pound of fruit weigh a pound of sugar; mash the fruit in a pan with a wooden spoon; put the sugar to it, and boil it hard for fifteen or twenty minutes.

To four pounds of raspberries you may add one pound of ripe currants; they give the jam a fine flavor and a pretty color.

Blackberry jam is made in the same manner; only leave out the currants.

GREEN GAGE JAM.

442. Wash the fruit, and stew it with enough water to keep them from scorching. Mash them, and strain the pulp through a colander. To a pint of pulp add a pound of sugar. When the sugar is dissolved, boil it till it is a smooth mass.

Plum jam is made in the same way.

PINE APPLE JAM.

443. This is made like all other jams, only the pine apple is grated.

BRANDY GRAPES.

444. Put some close bunches, when ripe, into

a jar, first pricking each grape with a needle; strew over them half their weight in pounded loaf sugar, fill up with brandy, and tie them closely. They look very handsome on the table.

BRANDY PEACHES.

445. Select the white cling-stone, known by the name of the "Heath peach." Make a hot ley of ashes and water, put in a few peaches at a time, and let them remain about a minute and a half, or until the skin will rub off with your finger. Take them out and throw them in a vessel of cold water, when all are done in this manner, rub off the skins with a cloth, and throw them in another vessel of cold water. Make a syrup of half a pound of sugar to a pound of fruit. Prepare it in the same manner as for preserves; put in your peaches, and let them boil until they are sufficiently tender to be easily pierced with a straw.

Take them out, and add to each pint of syrup a quart of the *very* **best** white brandy, when the fruit is cool put it in your jars, but leave plenty of room to fill them with the syrup, as if packed too closely they lose their shape.

SICK.

SAGO MILK.

446. Wash half an ounce of sago and soak it

in a tea cupful of cold water for an hour or more. Drain it and add to it three gills of good milk; put it over the fire and let it simmer until the sago is entirely incorporated with the milk. Sweeten it with white sugar. It may be flavored with vanilla, lemon, or nutmeg, if allowed of by the physician.

ORGEAT.

447. Blanch one ounce of bitter, and two of sweet almonds. Pound them in a mortar with a little milk until they are to a paste. Rub gradually into the pounded almond one tea cupful of milk. Sweeten it to the taste and strain it.

It may be flavored with lemon.

STEWED PRUNES.

448. Pour enough boiling water over your prunes to cover them, and stand them where they will keep hot but not boil. They require six or eight hours to cook. When they are perfectly done add sugar to the taste of the patient.

COCOA.

449. Put three table spoonsful of cocoa to a pint of water. Let it boil slowly for an hour. Put some sugar and cream in a bowl, pour the cocoa over it and serve hot with toast.

EGG AND WINE.

450. Beat the yelk of an egg very light, add to it a glass of wine and sugar to the taste.

SAGO PUDDING FOR INVALIDS.

451. See tapioca pudding, No. 452.

TAPIOCA PUDDING.

452. Pick and wash a table spoonful of tapioca, pour over it a pint of warm milk, and stand it near the fire for about one hour, but do not let it simmer. Then boil it until it forms a semi-transparent mucilage. Stand it aside to cool.

Beat two eggs, stir them into the mucilage with as much sugar as will sweeten it, pour the mixture in a pan and bake it slowly.

It may be eaten with sweet sauce.

Arrow-root and sago can be made in the same manner, only the sago requires more soaking and boiling than the tapioca.

ARROW-ROOT PUDDING FOR INVALIDS.

453. See tapioca pudding, No. 452.

PUDDING FOR THE CONVALESCENT.

454. One pint of milk,
    Two table spoonsful of flour,

Three eggs,
Sugar to the taste.

Beat the eggs, add the sugar, then the milk and flour by turns. Put the mixture in a bowl or pan, place it in another pan of hot water, set it where it will cook, and when a custard is formed set it off to cool.

There should not be too much sugar for invalids as it is apt to produce dispepsia.

INDIAN GRUEL.

455. Stir one table spoonful of Indian meal mixed with a little cold water into a pint of boiling water. Let it boil fifteen minutes and add salt to the taste.

EGG AND MILK.

456. Take a fresh egg, break it in a saucer, and with a three-pronged fork beat it until it is as thick as batter. Have ready half a pint of new milk sweetened with white sugar, stir the egg into the milk, and serve it with a piece of sponge-cake or slice of toast. It is considered very light, nourishing food for an invalid.

Some prefer the yelk and white of the egg beaten separately. The yelk should be beaten till it is very light and thick, then pour it into the sweetened milk; afterwards beat the white till it will stand alone, and add gradually half a tea spoonful of white sugar; pile the white on the top of the milk and serve as before.

SUGARED ORANGE.

457. Select the lightest colored oranges for this purpose, as they are more acid than the dark. Peel off the rind and slice them, latitudinally or crosswise, about the eighth of an inch in thickness. Strew over them some powdered white sugar, in the proportion of a tea spoonful of sugar to each slice. Let them stand fifteen minutes. They are very palatable in fevers, as they serve to cleanse the mouth and keep it cool.

SUGARED LEMONS, No. 1.

458. These may be prepared in the same manner as the sugared oranges (see above,) only they should have a tea spoonful and a half of sugar to each slice; as they are more firm than oranges, they require to stand longer to become perfectly impregnated with the sugar.

They are better to stand about an hour before they are to be eaten. The white skin should be carefully peeled off, as it imparts an unpleasant bitter flavor when permitted to remain long in the sugar. These are very grateful to the sick and feverish.

SUGARED LEMONS, No. 2.

459. Select fine large lemons. Peel off the outer skin and as much as possible of the white skin. Cut them in slices latitudinally or *round* the lemon, about the eight of an inch thick. Sprinkle them with white powdered sugar, a tea spoonful of sugar to each slice. Let them stand three hours, then strain off as much of the juice as possible from the lemons, put it in a sauce-pan over a slow fire, and as soon as the juice begins to simmer throw in the slices of lemon. Let them cook five minutes, take them out and pour the syrup over them. Should the lemons not prove sufficiently juicy to melt the sugar entirely, a little water may be added.

MULLED WINE.

460. Half a pint of wine,
Half a pint of water,
One egg,
Sugar and nutmeg to the taste.

Mix the wine and water together—let it boil. Beat the eggs in a pan, pour them into the wine, then quickly pour the whole from one vessel into another five or six times.

MULLED CIDER.

461. One pint of cider,

One egg,
Sugar and nutmeg to the taste.

Boil the cider. Have the egg well beaten, pour it into the cider, then have ready two vessels and pour the whole quickly from one vessel into the other several times. Add the sugar and nutmeg.

VEGETABLE SOUP.

462. Two potatoes,
Two onions,
Two turnips,
One carrot,
A little parsley chopped fine,
Salt to the taste.

Cut the potatoes in quarters, slice the onions, cut the turnips in quarters, slice the carrots. Put all in a stew-pan with three pints of water, and salt to the taste. Boil it down to one quart. About fifteen minutes before it is done add the parsley. Strain it and serve with light bread or toast.

This is the receipt of a late eminent physician of Philadelphia.

CARRAGEEN OR IRISH MOSS.

463. One ounce of moss,

One pint of water,
Lemon juice and sugar to the taste.

Boil the moss in water until it forms a jelly, and add the lemon-juice and sugar. Vanilla may be substituted for lemon-juice, but the latter is more palatable. Strain it.

ARROW ROOT.

464. One table spoonful of ground arrow-root,
One pint of water.

Mix the arrow-root with a little water, to the consistence of a paste. Have ready a pint of boiling water, pour the arrow-root into it, and let it boil till it looks clear; pour it off and sweeten to the taste. Some add a little lemon juice.

MACARONI.

465. Take a quarter of a pound of macaroni and boil it till it is very tender in water which has been salted. Take it up and drain it. If admissible a tea spoonful of melted butter may be poured over.

LEMONADE FOR AN INVALID.

466. Squeeze the juice out of a fine lemon, pour over it as much boiling water as will make it palatable, and add sugar to the taste. Stand it

away to cool; when cold it will be found quite as good as that made with cold water, and is generally preferred by physicians, as the boiling water destroys the unhealthy qualities of the lemon.

OAT-MEAL GRUEL.

467. Mix one table spoonful of oat-meal to a smooth paste with a little cold water. Pour this into one pint of boiling water; let it boil for half an hour.

Sweeten it and serve it with toast. Some prefer a little salt.

BAKED PUDDING FOR INVALIDS.

468. One pint of milk,
   Three eggs,
   Sugar to the taste,
   Two table spoonsful of flour.

Beat the eggs, add the sugar, then the flour, and stir in the milk gradually.

Butter a pan, pour in the pudding, and bake it.

CHICKEN BROTH.

469. Take half a chicken and pour over it three tea cupsful of cold water, with a salt spoonful of salt and two tea spoonsful of rice or pearl

barley. Let it simmer slowly until reduced to one half. Ten minutes before it is served, add some celery top, or parsley chopped very fine.

PAP OF UNBOLTED FLOUR.

470. Mix some unbolted flour with a little cold water, and stir it until it is smooth. Pour this into some boiling water, and let it boil fifteen or twenty minutes. Sweeten it and pour cream over it.

Children become very fond of this.

PAP OF GRATED FLOUR.

471. Take a quarter of a pound of flour and pour on just enough water to moisten it. Form it into a ball and tie it in a cloth, closely and firmly. Put it in a vessel of boiling water and let it boil the whole day. Then take it out, dip it in a pan of cold water, remove the cloth, and place it in a cool oven to dry, when it will be fit for use.

To make the pap, grate some of this, mix it to a paste with cold milk, and stir it into some boiling milk; boil it slowly ten or fifteen minutes.

SWEET-BREADS FOR INVALIDS.

472. Put them in a stew-pan, with just water sufficient to cover them, and very little salt.

Let them boil slowly until they are tender, but

not broken to pieces, then dish them, and if not quite salt enough, a little may be sprinkled over them. Care should be taken to season the meat for an invalid with very little salt, as it is frequently very unpalatable during convalescence.

After the sweet-breads have been cooked as above described, they may be taken from the water and drained; then heat the gridiron, grease the bars, to prevent the sweet-breads from sticking, and broil them quickly over some hot coals. They should be of a very delicate brown when done.

PANADA, No. 1.

473. Mix two tea spoonsful of grated cracker, with a little cold water, and stir it into half a pint of boiling water. Let it boil a few minutes till it thickens, then sweeten it with white sugar, and flavor it with wine and nutmeg to the taste.

Toast a slice of bread nicely, cut it in pieces about an inch square, put them in a bowl, and pour the panada over.

PANADA, No. 2.

474. Cut some light stale bread in small squares, put it in a bowl, and pour over some boiling water. Sweeten it to the taste with white sugar. Add wine and nutmeg if permitted by the physician.

Boiling milk may be substituted in place of the water if approved.

GROUND RICE, No. 1.

475. One table spoonful of ground rice,
One pint of milk.

Mix the rice with cold milk to a smooth paste. Set the pint of milk over the fire, and as soon as it boils, stir in the rice; let it boil for fifteen minutes, but be careful not to let it burn.

Sweeten it to the taste with white sugar; it may be flavored with vanilla if approved of.

GROUND RICE, No. 2.

476. Two table spoonsful of ground rice,
One pint of milk.

Boil the milk, and stir in the rice, which must have been previously mixed with cold milk.

Let it boil slowly twenty minutes; if it should be thicker than a thin batter, add a little more milk. Sweeten it to the taste.

Pour it into tea cups, and serve it with cream if allowed of by the physician.

MUSTARD WHEY.

477. Take two heaping tea spoonsful of mus-

tard seed, mash them a little, and pour over them six wine glasses of milk, boil it till the milk is curdled. Take it off the fire, let it stand to cool, and strain off the whey.

WINE WHEY.

478. Put a pint of milk over the fire, and the moment it boils stir into it two glasses of wine mixed with two tea spoonsful of sugar. Let it boil once again; stand it off to cool, and strain the whey through a fine strainer or sieve.

VINEGAR WHEY.

479. Half a gill of vinegar mixed with two tea spoonsful of sugar, stirred into two tea cupsful of boiling milk; let it boil one or two minutes, stand it off to cool, and strain off the whey. This is often recommended in fevers.

Lemon-juice may be used in place of the vinegar.

RENNET WHEY.

480. Wash a piece of rennet about the size of a dollar, and soak it for six hours or more in two table spoonsful of warm water. Pour this into three tea cupsful of lukewarm milk; let it stand near the fire until a thick curd is formed. With a knife break it in pieces and strain off the whey.

TAMARIND WHEY.

481. Stir half a wine glass of tamarinds mixed with three tea spoonsful of sugar into a pint of boiling milk; as soon as it boils stand it off the fire to cool, and strain off the whey.

POTATO JELLY.

482. Grate some white potatoes into cold water, stir it well, and strain it through a hair sieve. Let it stand a couple of hours, till the farina settles at the bottom, then pour the water off, and set the vessel on its side, so as all the water may drip out and the farina become perfectly dry.

Then put it into a box or jar for use.

Take a tea spoonful of this farina mixed smoothly in a little cold water, and pour as much boiling water over it as will make it a thick jelly. Let it boil two or three minutes, sweeten it to the taste, and flavor it with lemon or nutmeg. To be eaten cold.

Milk may be substituted for water.

PORT WINE JELLY.

483. Half an ounce of Russian isinglass,
    Half an ounce of gum arabic,
    One ounce of rock candy,
    Half a pint of boiling water,
    Half a pint of port wine.

Cut the isinglass in very small pieces, pound up the candy and gum arabic, pour the boiling water over, and stand it where it will keep hot but not simmer. When the above named ingredients are dissolved, add the wine, and boil the whole a few minutes.

Strain it and set it away to get cold.

TAPIOCA JELLY.

484. Soak a quarter of a pound of tapioca in water enough to cover it. Let it stand several hours, then stir it into a pint of boiling water. Simmer it slowly till it appears semi-transparent. Sweeten it to the taste, and flavor with wine and nutmeg if approved of by the physician. Turn it into cups or moulds.

HARTSHORN JELLY.

485. Take a quart of boiling water and pour it over three ounces of hartshorn shavings. Boil it until reduced to one-half the original quantity. Pass it through a fine sieve, sweeten it, and stir in a table spoonful of lemon-juice and three ounces of sugar with a glass of wine.

It is very good without the lemon-juice and wine.

RICE JELLY.

486. Pick and wash some rice, and pour enough

water over it to cover it. Let it soak for three hours. Then simmer it very slowly till the rice is entirely soft. Whilst it is hot sweeten it with white sugar, and flavor it with any thing you please. Strain it and pour it in a mould.

JELLY OF GELATINE.

487. Half an ounce of gelatine,
One quart of water,
The grated rind and juice of two fine lemons,
The whites of four eggs,
Sugar to the taste.

Pour a quart of boiling water over the gelatine, and stand it near the fire to keep hot until the gelatine is dissolved. Add the rind and juice of the lemon with the sugar (which must be loaf or pulverized white;) let it boil once, take it off, strain it, and when lukewarm add the beaten whites of four eggs with the shells (which must have been washed and wiped dry.) Strain it till the jelly is perfectly clear. Pour it in moulds and set it to cool.

SLIPPERY-ELM TEA.

488. Strip your slippery-elm in small pieces; take two table spoonsful of these pieces and pour over them two tea cups of boiling water. Let it stand until it becomes mucilaginous, then strain it.

FLAX-SEED TEA.

489. Pour two tea cups of boiling water over two table spoonsful of unground flax-seed. Cover the vessel, and stand it in a warm place until a mucilage is formed. Be careful to keep it closely covered, as it soon becomes stringy if exposed to the air. When sweetened and flavored with lemon-juice it is a very palatable drink.

The lemon-juice should be scalded.

VEAL TEA.

490. Cut one pound of a knuckle of veal in thin slices, pour over it a quart of cold water. Cover it, and let it simmer for an hour and a half.

When boiled to a jelly it will keep for three or four days, and may be used at any time by pouring over it a little boiling water and letting it stand near the fire. Add salt to the taste.

BEEF TEA.

491. One pound of beef,
One quart of cold water.

Cut the beef in thin slices, and pour on the water. Cover it and set it in a warm place for three-quarters of an hour, then put it over a slow fire where it will simmer for half an hour. Strain it, and serve it hot or cold as recommended by the physician.

Salt it to the taste.

ESSENCE OF BEEF.

492. Select some lean, tender beef, cut it in small pieces, put them in a bottle and cork it.

Set the bottle in a pot of cold water, let the water boil six hours. The heat of the water will extract all the juice from the beef in the bottle.

MUTTON TEA.

493. Slice one pound of mutton, remove all the fat, and add one quart of cold water. Cover it, place it near the fire for an hour, then simmer it for two hours, strain it, and serve it warm.

Add salt to the taste.

CHICKEN TEA.

494. Cut a quarter of a chicken in small pieces, take off the skin, and remove all the fat, add to it a pint of cold water; cover it, and let it simmer till reduced to one-half. Strain it, and serve warm with toast lightly browned.

Add salt to suit the patient's taste.

GUM ARABIC WATER.

495. Pour one pint of boiling water over two

table spoonsful of gum arabic; add lemon-juice and sugar to the taste. Stand it away to get cold.

TAMARIND WATER.

496. Pour half a pint of boiling water in a table spoonful of tamarinds. Stand it away to get cold. Pour off the water, and add sugar to the taste. If it should prove too acid, cold water may be added.

GRAPE WATER.

497. Put in a tumbler a table spoonful of grape jelly. Fill the tumbler with cold water.

MULLED WATER.

498. One egg,
Half a pint of boiling water,
Sugar to the taste.

Beat the egg well; pour the water gradually over it, but be sure to stir it all the time. Sweeten it to the taste of the patient.

Serve it with light bread or dry toast.

Wine may be added if approved of by the physician.

APPLE WATER.

499. Slice three large pippin apples, and pour

over them a pint of boiling water. Stand them in a cool place, when perfectly cold strain off the water, and sweeten it to the taste.

Toast may be added.

BARLEY WATER.

500. Wash and pick one ounce of pearl barley, pour over it one tea cupful of water, and let it boil for ten minutes. Drain it, and pour over it three tea cupsful of boiling water; set it over the fire, and boil it down one half. Strain it through a hair sieve or piece of muslin.

Gum arabic is sometimes dissolved in it; the liquid sweetened to the taste, forms a very agreeable drink.

TOAST WATER.

501. Toast two or three slices of bread of a dark brown all the way through, but do not burn it. Put the toast in a deep bowl, and pour over it one quart of water, let it stand for two or three hours. Then pour the water from the bread.

Some flavor it by soaking a piece of lemon-peel with the bread.

ALMOND WATER.

502. One ounce of sweet almonds (blanched,)
Half an ounce of white powdered sugar,
Three half pints of water.

Pour boiling water on the almonds, and in a few minutes the brown skin will come off by taking each kernel between the thumb and finger and gently pressing it. After having blanched them in this manner, put them in a stone or wedgewood mortar with the sugar and a little water. Add the water gradually until the almond is perfectly smooth. Strain it through a fine hair sieve or cloth.

More or less sugar may be added according to the taste.

MISCELLANEOUS.

LEMON SYRUP, No. 1.

503. Eight pounds of sugar,
　　Three quarts of water,
　　One quart of lemon-juice.

Mix the sugar and water together; as soon as the sugar has dissolved place it over the fire and boil and skim it, then add the lemon-juice.

LEMON SYRUP, No. 2.

504. Six pounds of sugar,
　　Two quarts of water,
　　One pint of lemon-juice.

Mix the sugar and water together, and as soon

as the sugar is dissolved place it over the fire; boil and skim it, then add the lemon-juice.

GINGER SYRUP.

505. One pound of green ginger root,
 Ten pounds of sugar,
 Two gallons of water.

Cut up the root in pieces and add to it two gallons of water; boil it till reduced to one gallon, strain it, and pour it over ten pounds of white sugar. When the sugar has dissolved boil and skim it till no more scum rises· take it off, and when cold bottle it for use.

BRANDY CHERRIES.

506. Stem your cherries, put them into a jar, and to a pound of fruit put a pound of white sugar. Cover them with French brandy and tie them closely.

Monongahela whisky will do as well as the brandy and is much cheaper.

TO PRESERVE EGGS DURING THE WINTER.

507. In the fall as you collect your eggs, pack them in a keg with a layer of salt at the bottom, then a layer of eggs, set in with the small end downwards, then a layer of salt, and so on till all are in; then put a layer of salt on the top.

BLACKBERRY CORDIAL.

508. Gather the ripest fruit, mash it in a pan with a large wooden spoon, strain out all the juice, and allow a quarter of a pound of sugar to a pint of the juice. Mix the juice and sugar together, and boil and skim it; then strain it again, and when cool to each pint of juice add a tea cupful of brandy. Bottle it and it will be fit for use. This is highly esteemed by some in cases of dysentery.

RASPBERRY BRANDY.

509. Pick the fruit when dry, put it into a glass jar, and place the jar in a kettle of cold water. Set the kettle over the fire and let the water get hot; let the fruit remain thus until the juice will run; strain it, and to every pint of juice add half a pound of sugar. Boil and skim it. When cold mix with it an equal quantity of brandy.

Bottle it tightly.

CURRANT SHRUB.

510. Mix a pound of sugar with every pint of currant-juice. When the sugar is dissolved boil it a few minutes and skim it. When almost cold add a gill of brandy to every quart of syrup.

Bottle it, cork it well, and keep it in a cool place.

RASPBERRY SHRUB.

511. This is made in the same manner as the currant shrub.

CHERRY BOUNCE.

512. To fifteen pounds of morella cherries add one gallon of the best French brandy or good Monongahela whisky. Let them stand for three or four months, then pour off the liquor and add to the cherries two quarts of water, which should remain on them for three weeks; pour off the water and add it to the liquor; to all of which add four pounds of sugar made into a syrup.

MIXTURE FOR SALTING BUTTER.

513. Half a pound of *fine* salt,
A quarter of a pound of *pulverized loaf sugar*.

Mix them well together, and add one ounce of the mixture to every pound of butter.

This is to keep butter sweet for winter use.

EGG-NOG.

514. Six eggs,
One pint of milk,
Half a pound of loaf sugar,
Half a pint of brandy.

Beat the eggs very light and thick, add the milk sugar and brandy.

MINCED MEAT.

515. Five pounds of beef or tongue,
   Two pounds of suet,
   Seven pounds of sugar,
   Seven pounds of apples,
   Three pounds of raisins,
   Three pounds of currants,
   Three nutmegs,
   Two ounces of cinnamon,
   A dessert spoonful of ground allspice,
   One small tea spoonful of ground mace,
   The juice of two lemons and the grated rind of one,
   Moisten it with equal portions of wine and cider,
   Brandy to the taste.

Boil the meat in water which has been salted in the proportion of one tea spoonful of salt to every quart of water. When it is tender stand it away to get perfectly cold before it is chopped. Wash, pick and dry your currants, prepare the spices, and seed the raisins. Pare and core the apples, chop them fine, chop the meat very fine, add the fruit, sugar and spice, lemon-juice, and grated lemon rind, (also the brandy and wine.) Mix the whole thoroughly; it will be fit for use on the following day. If you wish to keep your minced meat for several weeks, chop the meat and add the currants, raisins, sugar and spice, but leave out the apples, lemon, wine and cider; mix the other ingredients and merely moisten it with brandy; pack the mixture tightly in a stone jar and cover it close.

When you wish to make it into pies, take out some of the meat, chop your apples, and mix with it in the proportions given above. Moisten with cider, and add wine and brandy to your taste.

SANDWICHES.

516. These are generally made of cold boiled ham or tongue. Slice your ham or tongue as thin as possible. Then butter your bread on the loaf, and with a very sharp knife cut it in *very thin* slices. Roll in each slice of bread a slice of the ham or tongue. A cold fried oyster is very nice in each sandwich.

WINE SANGAREE.

517. Mix equal portions of wine and water, sweeten it to your taste, and grate nutmeg over the top.

Ale or porter sangaree is made in the same manner.

POACHED EGGS.

518. Have a broad shallow vessel of boiling water. Break your eggs in a plate, and be careful not to break the yelks. Take the water from the fire, slide the eggs carefully into it one at a time, and then put them over the fire again. Whilst they are boiling throw the water over the yelks with a spoon, and as soon as the whites are thick take them out with an egg slice. Trim them neatly and send them to the table hot.

PLAIN OMELETTE.

519. Beat four eggs very light. Have ready a pan of hot butter, pour the beaten eggs into it, and fry it till it is of a fine brown on the under side, then lap one half over the other, and serve it hot. Just before you lap it, sprinkle a little salt and pepper over the top.

Chopped parsley or onion may be mixed with the egg before it is fried.

HAM OMELETTE.

520. Whisk four eggs very light, and add to it as much grated ham as will flavor it. Fry it in hot butter till it is brown on the lower side. Sprinkle salt and pepper over it, and fold one half over the other. The salt should not be put in the egg, as it thins it.

Garnish the dish with green parsley.

BREAD OMELETTE

521. One gill of bread crumbs,
Eight eggs,
A gill and a half of cream,
Pepper and salt to the taste.

Warm the cream and pour it over a gill of baker's bread crumbs; when the bread is perfectly soft mash it well with the cream, and add pepper and salt to the taste. Beat the eggs and stir them into the bread and cream. Have a pan of hot butter, pour the mixture in and fry it. Do not turn it as that will make it heavy. The top may be browned with a salamander, or the pan of the shovel heated very hot and held near it will brown it. It may be folded one half over the other; in that case it need not be browned with a salamander.

TOMATO OMELETTE.

522. Six eggs,
A wine-glass of flour,
Four ripe tomatoes,
Pepper and salt to the taste,
Milk sufficient to mix the flour smoothly.

Beat the eggs very light, stir in the mixed milk and flour, peel and chop the tomatoes and add with the pepper and salt. Have a pan with some hot butter, pour in the mixture and fry it. When done it may be lapped half over or not, according to the fancy. Do not turn it.

BROWNED FLOUR.

523. This is very useful to thicken gravy and give it a brown color.

Put your flour into a pan, and set it over a moderate fire, stir it all the time till it is brown, but do not let it scorch, as it will communicate an unpleasant taste to your gravy.

When it is cool put it in a jar for future use.

DRIED CHERRIES, FOR PIES.

524. Pick your cherries, and wash them thoroughly through several waters to remove all the grit. Put them into a stone jar with half a pound of sugar to a pound of cherries, and warm water enough to cover them. Place your jar in a vessel of water and set it where it will keep hot. Let them stand for twelve hours. If the water should soak into the cherries and leave them too dry, add a little more. When they are fully swollen and perfectly soft they are fit for use. If they are not sweet enough add more sugar.

Dried fruits are more tender and juicy cooked in this manner than when they are boiled or stewed.

DRIED APPLES, FOR PIES.

525. Pick and wash them well. Then pour over boiling water enough to cover them. Let them stand all night to soak. In the morning put the apples with the water they were soaked in into your stew-pan, if they have absorbed all the water and are nearly dry, add a little more, simmer them slowly, but do not let them boil. When perfectly soft, pass them through a sieve, and prepare them for pies according to the directions given for apples which have not been dried.

DRIED PEACHES, FOR PIES.

526. These are cooked in the same manner as dried apples (see above,) only they are flavored with a piece of lemon or orange-peel stewed with them.

When they are done, take out the peel and mash them, add sugar to the taste. They require no butter.

DRIED PUMPKIN, FOR PIES

527. Cut a pumpkin in half lengthwise, take out the seeds, pare off the rind, and cut it in slices about an inch thick. String it on fine twine and hang it in a dry place.

In the winter stew and use it as green pumpkin. The cheese-shaped pumpkin is the best kind for drying.

TO PREPARE SALÆRATUS.

528. Put the salæratus in a vessel, add enough cold water to dissolve it, then pour off the liquid into a bottle and cork it. Be careful to pour it off gently as a great deal of sediment settles at the bottom of the vessel in which it is dissolved.

Carbonate of ammonia is much nicer than salæratus; it is prepared in the same manner; be careful to keep the bottle corked, and keep it in a cool place.

It may be used in all the receipts where salæratus is directed; but only half the quantity is necessary—thus: if one table spoonful of the salæratus is required, half a table spoonful of ammonia will be sufficient.

LEMONADE.

529. One quart of lemon-juice,
Nine quarts of water,
Eight pounds of white sugar.

Mix the lemon-juice and sugar, and stand it away. Just before the lemonade is served, add the water which should be iced.

PUNCH.

530. Four pounds of sugar,
One pint of lemon-juice,
One pint of Jamaica spirits,

Half a pint of peach brandy,
Half a pint of French brandy,
Five quarts of water.

The quantity of liquor may be regulated according to the taste.

MACARONI.

531. A quarter of a pound of macaroni,
One tea spoonful of butter,
One gill of milk or cream,
One table spoonful of grated cheese.

Boil the macaroni in water that has been salted in the proportion of a tea spoonful of salt to a quart of water. When it is tender take it out of the water and place it on a sieve, or in a colander, to drain. Boil a gill of milk or cream, and add to it a tea spoonful of butter rolled in flour, let it boil half a minute. Put your macaroni, after it is well drained, into a stew-pan, pour this boiled cream over it, and add to it the grated cheese. Let it get very hot, but do not let it boil, and serve it.

INDIAN MUSH.

532. Two quarts of water,
Two tea spoonsful of salt,
As much Indian meal as will make a thick batter.

Have a pot with two quarts of boiling water, add the salt as above, and stir in *very gradually* as much Indian meal as will form a thick batter. Let it boil half an hour, and beat it hard all the time it is cooking, which will make it light when done.

This is generally eaten with new milk, or sometimes with molasses and butter.

FRIED MUSH.

533. The mush is prepared as in the above receipt. Let it get cold, cut it in slices, flour them on both sides, and fry them of a light brown.

WELSH RABBIT.

534. Cut some old rich cheese in very thin pieces, add to it a spoonful of cream. Put it over a slow fire and let it stand until the cheese is entirely dissolved.

Serve it with toast. Some like pepper and mustard.

MINT JULEP.

535. Take young mint, pick off the leaves, wash them, and to one tumbler of leaves add one tumbler of brandy and Jamaica spirits mixed. Pour the liquor on the mint to extract the flavor, then strain it off on a tumbler of sugar; when the sugar

is dissolved, add a tumbler of ice finely pounded. Stir all well together.

MILK PUNCH.

536. Sweeten a half pint of rich milk to the taste. Add to this half a table spoonful of fourth proof brandy.

COTTAGE CHEESE.

537. Put some sour milk in a warm place until the whey begins to separate from the curd, but by no means let it get hard. Pour the curd into a three cornered bag in the shape of a pudding bag, hang it up and let it drain until no more water will drip from it. Then turn it out into a pan, mash the curd very fine and smooth with a wooden spoon; add as much good rich cream, as will make it about as thick as batter. Salt it to your taste. Sprinkle pepper over the top if you choose.

TO PREPARE RENNET.

538. Get a dried rennet in market, wash it in lukewarm water, but do not scrape it. Cut it up in small pieces, put them in a bottle, and pour over them a quart of Lisbon wine. After this has stood for a week a table spoonful of the wine will turn a quart of milk. Or if the use of wine is objectionable, the rennet may be preserved by hanging it in a

cool dry place. And then every time you wish to use it, cut off a piece, wash it, and soak it in warm water; the water it is soaked in will turn the milk.

TO CURE HAMS.

539. The following is the Newbold receipt for curing hams.

    Seven pounds of coarse salt,
    Five pounds of brown sugar,
    Half an ounce of pearl-ash, two ounces of saltpetre,
    Four gallons of water.

Boil the above ingredients together, and skim the pickle when cold. Pour it over your hams, and let them remain in it eight weeks.

The above proportions are for one hundred pounds of meat.

TO PREPARE APPLES FOR PIES.

540. Pare and core your apples, cut them in slices, and throw them into cold water. Then take them out of the water, put them into a stew-pan; if the apples are tender, the water which adheres to them will be sufficient to cook them; if not, a little more may be added. Cover the stew-pan, and place them near the fire. Let them stew till they are soft and burst; then mash them, and add half an ounce of butter to each pint of the stewed ap-

ple. When they get nearly cold, add sugar, rose-water, and nutmeg to the taste.

TO CURE DRIED BEEF.

541. For one hundred pounds of beef:
Seven pounds of coarse salt,
Five pounds of brown sugar,
Half an ounce of pearl-ash, two ounces of saltpetre. Four gallons of water

Boil the sugar, salt, pearl-ash, saltpetre and water together, skim it and pour it over the meat when it is cold. At the end of three weeks take out your beef. This is the celebrated Newbold receipt.

TO CURE BEEF AND HAMS.

542. Half a bushel of fine salt,
Half a pound of saltpetre,
Half a gallon of molasses.

Mix the salt, saltpetre, and molasses together well with your hands, until the mixture resembles brown sugar.

Rub the meat well with this mixture, then place it in your tubs, with the fleshy side up; it should have a coating of the salt, &c., at least half an inch thick. At the end of ten days, or two weeks at farthest, take out your beef, and hang it in a dry place. Hams should remain in the salt from five to six weeks.

Never smoke beef. Hams would be better if not smoked.

TO CURE SHAD.

543. Clean the shad nicely, place them in layers with back down, and laid open so as the inside of the fish may be up. Sprinkle each fish plentifully with ground salt, and let them stand twenty-four hours. This draws out all the blood. Wipe them all dry with clean napkins.

Place them in layers in a clean tub, with the backs down as before. For one hundred shad take half a pound of saltpetre, and two pounds of brown sugar. Strew plenty of rock salt over them with the saltpetre and sugar, there is no danger of putting on too much salt as they will only absorb a certain quantity.

TO ROAST COFFEE.

544. Pick the black or imperfect grains from the coffee. Put it in a pan, and stir it all the time it is roasting; when done it should be the color of the hull of a ripe chestnut. It should be brown all through, but not black. About ten minutes before it is done add to two pounds of coffee half

an ounce of butter. Whilst hot put it in a box and cover it closely.

COFFEE.

545. Beat an egg; and to one tea cupful of ground coffee add one-third of the beaten egg, and as much cold water as will just moisten the coffee; do not put in much cold water, stir all well together, put the mixture in your coffee pot, and pour over it six tea cupsful of *boiling* water. Let it boil hard for ten or fifteen minutes. When it begins to boil stir it frequently, and never leave it until the grounds sink, which they will do in a few minutes after it has been on the fire. Be careful and do not let your coffee boil over, as by that means you lose a great deal of the grounds and consequently the coffee will be weakened.

Rinse your pot, if it be silver or britania metal, with *boiling water*, pour the coffee into it, and serve it hot. Coffee and tea lose much of their flavor if served cold.

CHOCOLATE.

546. Shave down three ounces of chocolate, over this pour enough hot water to dissolve it; mix it to a smooth paste, put it in a pipkin, and add one quart of boiling water. Place it on the fire, stir it occasionally, and let it boil fifteen

minutes, then add one tea cupful of rich milk or cream. Let it boil a minute or two longer, pour it off, and send it to the table. Chocolate retains its heat longer than either tea or coffee.

Never boil chocolate in your coffee pot as it would be likely to impart to the coffee an unpleasant flavor.

TEA.

547. Scald your tea pot with boiling water, and allow a tea spoonful of tea for each person and one over. Pour enough boiling water on the tea leaves to rather more than wet them. Let it stand fifteen minutes; pour on as much boiling water as will serve one cup to each one of the company. As soon as the first cups are poured out, add half a tea spoonful for each person, and pour on some boiling water. The most convenient article for hot water is an urn with an iron heater inside which keeps it boiling on the table. But water may be kept sufficiently hot in an ordinary tea pot.

Some who are particular about their tea, stop the spout of the tea pot with a cork, while the tea is drawing, to retain the aroma.

Tea and coffee pots should always be set away with the lids off.

TO MAKE YEAST.

548. Boil a tea cupful of hops in one quart of

water till reduced to one half. Strain it through a sieve, and add one wine glassful of salt. Return the hot water into the vessel it was boiled in. Mix some flour with cold water, and stir in so as to make it about the consistency of thick molasses. Let it boil a few minutes, then take it off the fire, and set it away to cool; when lukewarm, add some yeast, and when it rises put it into a stone jar; which should not be filled, cover it, and the following day it will be fit for use.

As the yeast is so well salted there is no necessity to put salt in the bread.

You should always have a vessel on purpose to boil hops.

POTATO YEAST.

549. Boil some potatoes, mash them, and to six potatoes add one gill of flour. Stir in as much water as will make the whole into a thick batter; add some yeast and a wine glassful of salt. When it is light, put it in your jar and cover it.

BREAD.

550. Set a sponge at night of a pound of flour, a little salt, if your yeast should not be salt enough, a gill of yeast, and water enough to make a thick batter. In the morning stir in as much flour as will form a dough, knead it well, and if the weather is cold set it in a warm place to rise. When

it is light grease your pans, mould out the dough in loaves, put them in the pans, and as soon as they rise again bake them.

If the weather is cold, set your sponge with lukewarm water, place it near the fire to rise. But in summer it should be set with cold water, and not be placed near the fire. It is better in warm weather to put the dough in your pans as soon as the flour is added to the sponge and the dough well kneaded, as if permitted to stand it might turn sour.

Bread is much nicer baked in small loaves.

POTATO BREAD.

551. Boil some potatoes, mash them fine, and add as much warm water as will make a mixture about as thick as cream. Pass it through a sieve in order to extract all the lumps. When cool add a little salt, some yeast, and as much flour as will make a very thick batter.

The next morning stir in enough flour to make a dough. Knead it well, let it rise, when light grease your pans, mould it out gently into loaves, put them in the pans, let them stand till they rise again, then bake them.

This bread may be made with milk instead of water, but it is best when eaten fresh, as it soon becomes dry.

MUSH BREAD.

552. Make some thin Indian mush, (see No. 532,) when cool add a little salt and flour enough to make a thick batter, stir in some yeast.

Let it stand all night to rise, in the morning add flour enough to form a dough. Knead it well, set it to rise; when light mould it out in loaves, grease your pans, and when it gets light again bake it.

RYE BREAD.

553. This is made in the same manner as wheat, (No. 550,) only it must have more rye flour to make a stiffer dough, and requires more kneading. It takes rather longer to bake than wheat bread.

DYSPEPTIC BREAD.

554. This bread is made of unbolted flour instead of that in general use.

It is made in the same manner as bread, (No. 550,) knead it very well and be careful to have it thoroughly baked.

Toast made of this bread is very good.

FRIED BREAD.

555. Slice some bread, stale is better than fresh; pour over it enough rich milk or cream, if you have it, to moisten it. Beat an egg, dip each

slice of the bread in the egg, and fry them brown on both sides. Season the bread with pepper and salt to your taste.

COMMON MUSTARD.

556. One table spoonful of ground mustard.
One tea spoonful of sugar,
One salt spoonful of salt.

Mix the salt, sugar, and mustard together, and then pour on some boiling water gradually, stir it with a horn spoon or knife till it is quite smooth. Some like it quite thick, others prefer it so thin as to run on the plate.

ICING FOR CAKES.

557. Beat the whites of two eggs till they are very dry, then add gradually ten ounces of pulverized white sugar. Dredge flour over the top of the cake and wipe it off, to make the icing adhere. Put it over with a broad bladed knife; it should be put on quite thick. When this coating is dry, dilute the remainder of the icing on your dish with a little rose-water, and put another coating over the top, which will have a glossy appearance.

TO DRY HERBS.

558. They should be picked just before the

plant blossoms, wash them to free them from the dust, place them on a sieve to drain. Then put them in the oven after the bread has been drawn out, and let them remain in it till they are perfectly dry. Rub them from the stalks, put them in glass jars and cover them closely.

RASPBERRY VINEGAR.

559. Take ripe raspberries, put them in a pan, and mash them with a large wooden spoon or masher. Strain the juice through a jelly bag, and to each pint of juice add one pound of loaf sugar and one quart of vinegar. When the sugar has dissolved place the whole over the fire in a preserving kettle, and let it boil a minute or two and skim it. When cold bottle it, cork it well, and it will be fit for use.

CELERY VINEGAR.

560. Put half a pint of celery seed into a quart of vinegar; bottle it, and in a month it will be fit for use. It must be strained before it is put in the castor bottle.

PEPPER VINEGAR.

561. Put the coral peppers in a bottle, and pour over vinegar enough to cover them.

MOLASSES CANDY.

562. One quart of West India molasses,
Half a pound of brown sugar,
The juice of one lemon.

Put the molasses in a kettle with the sugar, boil it over a slow, steady fire till it is done, which you can easily tell by dropping a little in cold water, if done it will be crisp, if not, it will be stringy. A good way to judge if it is boiled enough is to let it boil till it stops bubbling. Stir it very frequently, and just before it is taken off the fire add the lemon-juice. Butter a shallow tin pan, and pour it in to get cold.

Molasses candy may be flavored with any thing you choose. Some flavor with lemon, and add roasted ground-nuts, or almonds blanched.

GOOSEBERRY PIE.

563. Pick off the stems and blossoms of your gooseberries, wash them, and pour enough boiling water over to cover them. Let them stand a few minutes and then drain them. Line your pie-plates with paste, fill them with the fruit, and add three-quarters of a pound of sugar to a pint of fruit. Dredge a little flour over the top and cover with a lid of paste, leave an opening in the centre to permit the steam to escape, and bake them.

RIPE CURRANT PIE.

564. Stem your currants and wash them. Line your pie-plates with paste, fill them with the fruit, and add sugar in the proportion of a half a pound to one pint of currants. Dredge some flour over the top, put on the lid of the pie, leave an opening in the centre and bake it.

GREEN CURRANT PIE.

565. The fruit should have attained its full size before it is picked. Stem the currants and wash them; then pour enough boiling water over them to cover them, and let them stand while you prepare the paste. Line the bottom of your pie-plates with paste, drain your fruit through the colander and fill your plates, adding half a pound of sugar to a pint of currants, or in that proportion. Dredge a little flour over the fruit, and put on the top crust; leave an opening in the centre to permit the steam to escape. The pie requires no water, as a sufficient quantity will adhere to the fruit.

APPLE BUTTER.

566. Boil one barrel of cider till reduced to one half the original quantity. Pare, core, and slice enough apples to measure two bushels and a half when cut up. Put them in with the cider, let them boil, and stir it all the time it is boiling. The ap-

ples must be reduced to a pulp, which will take from nine to twelve hours. It should be boiled till perfectly smooth and thick. Great care should be taken not to let it scorch, as it would be entirely spoiled.

New cider is the kind used for making apple butter.

JELLY CAKE, No. 1.

567. Ten eggs,
　One pound of sugar,
　Three-quarters of a pound of sifted flour,
　The grated rind of two, and juice of one lemon.

Beat the yelks of the eggs very light and add the sugar. Stir the yelks and sugar very hard until they are smooth and light. Add to this the grated rind and lemon-juice, and beat it for a few minutes longer. Whisk the whites to a dry froth, and stir them in very gently. Do not beat it after the whites are in. Butter some shallow tin-plates and put in three table spoonsful of the mixture. Bake them in a quick oven. Or you may heat a griddle or bake-iron, grease it well with butter; grease a tin cake-ring, place the ring on the griddle, pour in three table spoonsful of the mixture, put the griddle in a hot oven, and bake it without turning it. When done take it off, grease the griddle and ring again, and proceed as before. When the cakes are cool place one on a plate, cover the top of it with any kind of *thick* jelly, put another cake on the top of this, cover it with a layer of jelly, and so on. Place the cakes evenly over each other. It is customary to ice the top one, though it looks very nice with white sugar sifted over.

These are better to be eaten fresh.

JELLY CAKE, No. 2.

568. One pound of flour,
   One pound of sugar,
   Three-quarters of a pound of butter,
   Ten eggs,
   One gill of rose-water,
   One tea spoonful of grated nutmeg,
   Half a tea spoonful of ground cinnamon.

Beat the butter and sugar to a cream, whisk the eggs very light and add to it; stir in the spices and rose-water, then the flour. Beat the mixture very hard for ten minutes. Heat your griddle or bake-iron, grease it well with butter, grease a cake-ring and place on the griddle. Pour into the ring three table spoonsful of the mixture, place the griddle in a hot oven and bake it quickly. These cakes are never turned; the oven should be hot enough to bake the top.

When one is done take it out, place it on a clean napkin to cool, and grease the griddle and ring and proceed as before. When they are all cold spread the top of each one with thick jelly, and place them neatly one over the other. The top cake should have no jelly on it. It may be iced, or have white sugar sifted over it.

HONEY CAKE, No 1.

569. Three-quarters of a pound of butter,
Three-quarters of a pound of sugar,
Six eggs,
Two pounds of flour,
One table spoonful of ground cinnamon,
Half a gill of cream,
One quart of honey,
One table spoonful of *dissolved* salæratus.

Beat the butter and sugar to a cream; beat the eggs and stir in with the flour, cinnamon, cream and honey. Beat the whole for ten minutes, then stir in the salæratus. Line your pan with several thicknesses of paper, well buttered; pour in the mixture and bake it in a slow oven.

HONEY CAKE, No. 2.

570. Half a pound of sugar,
Half a pound of butter,
One pint of honey,

One table spoonful of cinnamon,
One tea spoonful of nutmeg,
As much flour as will form a dough.

———

Stir the butter and sugar together, add the nutmeg, cinnamon, honey, and enough flour to form a dough. Knead it well, roll it out in sheets, cut it in cakes with a cake-cutter or the rim of a tumbler, place them on tins and bake them in a moderately hot oven. Before you set them in the oven wash them over with a little honey and water, mixed in equal quantities.

CITRON CAKE.

571. One pound of butter,
One pound of sugar,
One pound of flour,
One pound of citron,
Ten eggs,
Half a gill of brandy,
One tea spoonful of grated nutmeg,
One tea spoonful of cinnamon.

———

Grate the nutmeg, slice the citron in very thin narrow strips about half an inch long, and flour it. Beat the butter and sugar to a cream, whisk the eggs very light, and stir them in with the flour, brandy, and spices. Beat the whole for several minutes, then stir in the citron. Line your pans with several thicknesses of paper, well buttered, pour in the mixture and bake them in a slow oven. When cold ice them.

VANILLA KISSES.

572. Half a pound of pulverized white sugar,
   The whites of six eggs,
   One vanilla bean.

Pound the bean in a mortar until it is completely pulverized. Whisk the eggs to a stiff froth, add the sugar very gradually, then stir in the vanilla. Drop the mixture on white paper so as not to touch each other. You may make them any size you choose. About a dessert spoonful makes a pretty sized cake. Take care to have them sufficiently far apart. Place them on tins with several thicknesses of stout paper under them, set them in a hot oven, and as soon as they have a tinge of brown take them out, with a broad bladed knife slip them off the paper, and place the under sides of two together.

VANILLA CAKE.

573. Half a pound of pulverized white sugar,
   The whites of four eggs,
   One small vanilla bean, or half of a large one.

Pound the vanilla bean in a mortar until it is

completely pulverized. Beat the eggs to a dry froth, add the sugar very gradually; when all the sugar is in stir in the vanilla. Drop a tea spoonful of the mixture on thick white paper to form each cake, they must not be near enough to touch each other. Place them in a cool oven, and as soon as they are sufficiently dry take them out, as soon as they are cold slip the blade of a case-knife under each one to loosen it from the paper. The oven should not be hot enough to brown them.

GINGER POUND CAKE.

574. Three-quarters of a pound of butter,
Three-quarters of a pound of sugar,
Six eggs,
One pound and a half of flour,
One pint of molasses,
The grated rind of two large oranges,
Three table spoonsful of ginger,
Two table spoonsful of cinnamon,
One table spoonful of dissolved salæratus, or
One large tea spoonful of dissolved carbonate of ammonia.

Beat the butter and sugar to a cream. Beat the eggs very light and add to it, then stir in all the other ingredients except the salæratus or ammonia. Beat the mixture very hard for several minutes, then stir in the salæratus or ammonia. Butter an earthen cake mould or thick iron pan, pour in the mixture and bake it in a moderate oven. If you bake it in an iron pan line the pan with several thicknesses of stout paper well buttered.

CURRANT BISCUITS.

575. One pound of sugar,
One pound of butter,
One pound and a half of flour,
Four eggs,
One tea spoonful of cinnamon,
One tea spoonful of nutmeg.
One pound of currants.

Beat the butter and sugar together; whisk the eggs, and add to it with the other ingredients. Roll the dough out in sheets, cut it it into cakes, place them on tins, sift white sugar over the top, and bake them in a moderate oven.

The currants must first be picked, washed and dried, before they are put in the cakes.

PLAIN CRULLERS.

576. Three-quarters of a pound of pulverized white sugar,
Eight eggs,
As much flour as will make a soft dough,
One dessert spoonful of dissolved salæratus,
One tea spoonful of nutmeg,

One tea spoonful of cinnamon,
The grated rind of one lemon, or
Six drops of essence of lemon.

Whisk the eggs very light, stir in the sugar, and about half the flour, spices and lemon; then add the salæratus, and as much more flour as will make a soft dough. Do not knead it, but roll it with your hands in round strips, cut them about three inches long, double and twist them. Throw them into boiling lard to cook them. They require to be turned over whilst they are boiling in the lard, in order to have them brown on both sides. These cakes are very much liked and are very easily made. Sift sugar over before they are sent to the table.

TO MAKE BUTTER.

577. Strain your milk and stand it in a spring-house or cellar, which should be about 54° of Farenheit. The spring-house should be well ventilated. Let the milk stand about three days, then skim off the cream with a skimmer made for the purpose, and take care to get as little of the sour milk with it as possible. Then churn it; and after churning, wash your butter thoroughly in clear fresh water, which should be as cold as you can get it. Then salt it and work it well, to get out all the remaining buttermilk. It should be dry

and solid when you have finished working it this time. After your butter has been salted and worked thorougly, let it stand about five or six hours, or until every particle of salt is entirely dissolved; then work it again in order to mix the salt more completely through the whole mass, but do not touch it with your hands as it will make it greasy, and spoil both its appearance and taste. Make it into pounds or small prints, and it will be ready for use.

When more than one churning is done at a time, each churning should be worked separately, or it will be apt to be streaked; as, if the temperature of the cream is higher in one churning than in the other, the butter will not mix without appearing clouded.

The above receipt was obtained from one of the best butter-makers in Montgomery county, Pennsylvania, and may be confidently relied on for its accuracy.

QUEEN CAKE.

578. One pound of butter,
One pound of sugar,
Fourteen ounces of flour,
Ten eggs,
One tea spoonful of cinnamon,
One tea spoonful of nutmeg,

One large table spoonful of brandy,
One table spoonful of rose water.

Beat the butter and sugar to a cream, whisk the eggs well, and stir the whole together, add gradually the liquor, spices and flour. Beat the mixture for several minutes, butter some small round tin pans, fill them about three parts full and bake them.

Queen cakes are very nice with a few dried currants in them. To the above quantity one pound and a half of dried currants would be sufficient.

THE END.

INDEX.

A.

Almond cake, 191.
    pudding, 127.
    water, 253.
Apple cream, 163.
Apees, 217.
Apples, to prepare for pies, 268.
    baked, 160.
    dried, for pies, 263.
Apple dumplings, 136.
    floating island, 154.
    fritters, 157.
    pudding, No. 1, 129.
        No. 2, 130.
    pudding, plain, No. 3, 130.
    sauce, 101.
    water, 252.
Arrow-root, 241.
    pudding, for invalids, 236.
Asparagus, 96.

B.

Baked apples, 160.
    beef and Yorkshire pudding, 39.
    beets, 85.
    fillet of veal, 46.
    pears, 160.
    pudding, for invalids, 242.
    rabbit-pie, 61.
    shad, 24.
    tomatoes, 84.
Barley water, 253.
Beans, boiled dried, 99.
    Lima, 98.
    pickled, 113.
    stringed, 98.
    Windsor, or horse, 98.
Beef, a-la-mode, 38.
    and hams, to cure, 269.

Beef, boiled corned, **43.**
    corned, 42.
    essence of, 251.
Beef's kidney, stewed, **41.**
    fried, 42.
Beef steaks, 38.
    fried, 39.
    stewed with onions, **41.**
    soup, 15.
    tea, 250.
    to cure dried, **269.**
Beets, baked, 85.
    pickled, 117.
Best way of cooking **venison, 60.**
Biscuits, currant, 286.
    Dover, 218.
Biscuit, hard, 164.
    light sugar, **215.**
    Maryland, **167.**
    milk, 177.
    soda, 200.
    sugar, 220.
    travelers', 215.
    Yorkshire, 165.
Blackberry cordial, 256.
    jam, 233.
    mush, 160.
Blancmange, 150.
    clear, 150.
Boiled chickens, 74.
    cod, 22.
    corned **beef, 43.**
    crabs, 34.
    custard, 159.
    dried beans, 99.
    green **corn, 89.**
    ham, 58.
    leg of lamb, 52.
    lobster, 35.
    onions, 97.
    potatoes, No. 1, 78.
        No. 2, 79.
    pudding, No. 1, 145.

Boiled pudding, No. 2, 146.
    rice pudding, 144.
    rock, 21.
    shad, 23.
    sour-krout, 91.
    sweet-breads, 49.
    tongue, 43.
    turkey, 69.
Boston ginger-bread, 198.
Brandy cherries, 255.
    grapes, 233.
    peaches, 234.
    raspberry, 256.
Bread, 273,
    dyspeptic, 275.
    fried, 275.
    mush, 275.
    omelette, 261.
    potato, 274.
    rye, 275.
Brentford rolls, 166.
Bristol loaf-cake, 190.
Broiled chickens, 73.
    shad, 24.
    squab, 65.
    tomatoes, 84.
Browned egg-plant, 88.
    flour, 262.
Brown fricassee, 75.
Buckwheat cakes, 169.
Buns, 209.
    Guernsey, 170.
    Spanish, 209.
Butter, to make, 287.
    mixture for salting, 257.
Butter-milk cakes, 180.

C.

Cakes, 182.
    almond, 191.
    Bristol loaf, 190.
    buckwheat, 169.
    butter-milk, 180.
    cocoa-nut, 208.
        pound, 188.
    cod-fish, 23.
    common pound, 187.
    composition, 212.
    cream-of-tartar, 181.
    crumpets, or flannel, 171.

Cake, currant, 204.
    Devonshire, 205.
    election, 205.
    federal, 202.
    French, 213.
    fruit, or plum, No. 1, 183.
        No. 2, 184.
    German, 203.
    ginger cup, 196.
        fruit, 196.
        pound, 285.
    icing for, 276.
    Indian light, 175.
        loaf, 191.
        meal breakfast, 176.
        pound, 189.
    Johnny, or journey, 174.
    kisses, or cream, 200.
    lady, 211.
    loaf, 189
    mush, 179.
    New York plum, 185.
    parsnip, 167.
    plain cup, 216.
    potato, 81.
    pound, No. 1, 186.
        No. 2, 187.
    queen, 288.
    rice cup, 208.
    rock, 204.
    rye batter, 170.
    Scotch, 206.
    seed, 203.
    short, 163.
    Shrewsbury, 217.
    sponge, No. 1, 192.
        No. 2, 193.
        No. 3, 193.
    sugar, 201.
    tea, 163.
    vanilla, 284.
    Washington, No. 1, 218.
        No. 2, 219.
    white cup, 202.
Calves' feet, spiced, 59.
    fried, 50.
    liver, fried, 50.
Calf's-foot jelly, 222.
Caper sauce, 107.
Carrots, 95.
Carrageen, or Irish moss, 240

INDEX.

Cat-fish, 27.
Catsup, tomato, No. 1, 117.
    No. 2, 118.
    mushroom, 119.
    walnut, 119.
Cauliflower, 91.
Celery, dressed as slaw, 95.
    stewed with lamb, 96.
    vinegar, 277.
Charlotte, cherry, 153.
    peach, 152.
    de Russe, 151.
    Savoy, 152.
Cheese, cottage, 267.
Cheese-cake, cottage, 125.
    curd, 125.
    lemon, 124.
    orange, 123.
Chocolate, 271.
Chow chow, 112.
Cherry bounce, 257.
    Charlotte, 153.
    jam, 232.
    pie, 137.
Cherries, brandy, 255.
    dried, for pies, 262.
    pickled, 117.
Chickens, boiled, 74.
    broiled, 73.
    broth, 242.
    fried, 74.
    pie, 72.
    pot-pie, 73.
    roast, 72.
    salad, No. 1, 76.
    No. 2, 77.
    soup, 18.
    stewed, 75.
    tea, 251.
    white fricasseed, 76.
Chitterlings, or calves' tripe, 51.
Citron melon, preserved, 230.
Clams, fried, 33.
    stewed, 32.
    fritters, 32.
    soup, 19.
Clear blanc mange, 150.
Cocoa, 235.
Cocoa-nut cake, 208.
    jumbles, 195.

Cocoa-nut pound-cake, 188.
    pudding, No. 1, 128.
    No. 2, 128.
Cod, boiled, 22.
    fish cakes, 23.
Coffee, 271.
    to roast, 270.
Cold custard, 162.
    slaw, 92.
College pudding, 149.
Common ginger-bread, 199.
    mustard, 276.
    paste, 122.
    pound-cake, 187.
Composition cake, 212.
Cordial, blackberry, 256.
Corned beef, 42.
Corn, boiled green, 89.
    fritters, 80.
    oysters, 90.
    salad, 97.
    soup, 19.
Cottage cheese, 267.
    cheese-cake, 125.
Crabs, boiled, 34.
    soft, 34.
Cranberry jelly, No. 1, 223.
    No. 2, 224.
    sauce, 103.
    tarts, 134.
Cream, apple, 163.
    sauce, 104.
    of tartar cakes, 181.
Crumpets, or flannel cakes, 171.
    Scotch, 172.
Crullers, 206.
    plain, 286.
Cucumbers, fried, 98.
    pickled, 115.
Cup-cake, plain, 216.
    rice, 208.
Curd, cheese-cake, 125.
Currant biscuits, 286.
    cake, 204.
    glazed, 161.
    jelly, 225.
    shrub, 256.
Custard, boiled, 159.
    cold, 162.
    snow, 159.
    vanilla cup, 156.

Cutlets, veal, 47.
Cymlins, 94.

D.

Dandelion, 94.
Devonshire cake, 205.
Dough-nuts, 210.
Dover biscuits, 218.
Drawn butter, 105.
Dried apples, for pies, 263.
    beans, boiled, 99.
    beef, to cure, 269.
    cherries, for pies, 262.
    peaches, for pies, 263.
    peach sauce, 102.
    pumpkin, for pies, 263.
Duck, roasted, No. 1, **69.**
    No. 2, **70.**
Dumplings, apple, 136.
    peach, 136.
    quince, **136.**
    rice, 161.
Dutch loaf, 207.
    salad, 96.
Dyspeptic bread, **275.**

E.

Eggs, to preserve during winter, 255.
Egg and milk, **237.**
    wine, **236.**
  nog, 257.
  pickled, 111.
  plant, No. 1, 86.
    No. 2, 86
    No. 3, 86.
    No. 4, 87.
    No. 5, 87.
  plant, browned, 88
  poached, 260.
  sauce, 105.
Election cake, 205.
Essence of beef, 251.
Eve's pudding, 138.

F.

Farmers' apple pudding, 142.
Federal cake, 202.

Figs, preserved fresh, **230**
Fillet of veal a-la-mode, **46.**
Fish, 21.
Flax-seed tea, 250.
Floating island, 155.
    apple, **154.**
Florendines, Indian, 126.
    rice, 126.
Fox-grape jelly, 222.
French bread-pudding, **140.**
    cake, 213.
    custard pudding, **133.**
    pudding, 139.
    rolls, 166.
    slaw, 92.
    stew, No. 1, 40.
      No. 2, 41.
    stewed rabbit, 63.
    stew of veal, 47.
    tomato sauce, 108
Fricassee brown, 75.
    chicken white, **76.**
    rabbit, 63.
Fried beef's kidney, **42.**
    beef steak, 39.
    bread, 275.
    calves' liver, 50.
      feet, 50.
    chickens, 74.
    clams, 33.
    cucumbers, 98.
    mush, 266.
    oysters, 28.
    potatoes, No. 1, 79.
      No. 2, 80.
      No. 3, 80.
      No. 4, 80.
    reed birds, 67.
    rock, 22.
    shad, 24.
    sweet-breads. 49.
      potatoes, 80.
    tomatoes, 83.
    veal with tomatoes, **48.**
Fritters, apple, 157.
    clam, 32.
    corn, 89.
    Indian, 172.
    orange, 158.
    oyster, 30.
    Spanish, 157.

Fruit or plum-cake, No. 1, 183.
    No. 2, 184.
  cake, ginger, 196.

G.

Gelatine, jelly of, 249.
German cake, 203.
    puffs, 158
Giblet pie, 71.
Ginger-bread, No. 1, 198.
    No. 2, 198.
    Boston, 198.
    common, 199.
    plain, 199.
  cup-cake, 196.
  fruit-cake, 196.
  nuts, 197.
  pound-cake, 285.
  syrup, 255.
Glazed currants, 161.
  ham, 59.
  strawberries, 162.
Gooseberry pie, 278.
Goose, roast, 70.
Grape water, 252.
Green corn pudding, 141.
  soup, 19.
  currant pie, 279.
  gage jam, 233.
  gages, preserved, 231.
  peas, 99.
Ground rice, No. 1, 245.
    No. 2, 245.
Gruel, Indian, 237.
  oat-meal, 242.
Guernsey buns, 170.
    pudding, 137.
Gum-arabic water, 251.

H.

Halibut, 26.
Hams, to cure, 268.
Ham, boiled, 58.
  glazed, 59.
  omelette, 260.
Hard biscuit, 164.
Hartshorne jelly, 248.
Haslet sauce, 107.
Hasty pudding, or farmers' rice, 156.

Herbs, to dry, 276.
Herring, potted, 27.
Hog's-head cheese, 58.
Hominy, 90.
Horse beans, 98.
  radish sauce, 109.
Hot slaw, 92.

I.

Icing for cakes, 276.
Indian baked pudding, 147.
  boiled " 146.
  florendines, 126.
  fritters, 172.
  gruel, 237.
  light-cake, 175.
  loaf-cake, 191.
  meal breakfast cakes, 176.
  metland, 181.
  muffins, No. 1, 175.
    No. 2, 176.
  mush, 265.
  pone, 174.
  pound-cake, 189.
  slappers, 173.

J.

Jam, blackberry, 233.
  cherry, 232.
  green-gage, 233.
  pine-apple, 233.
  raspberry, 233.
  strawberry, 232.
Jelly, calf's foot, 222.
  currant, 225.
  fox-grape, 222.
  of gelatine, 249.
  hartshorn, 248.
  orange, 224.
  potato, 247.
  port wine, 247.
  quince, 226.
  rice, 248.
  strawberry, 225.
  tapioca, 248.
Jewish method of preparing beef for salting, 43.
Johnny, or journey cake, 174.
Jumbles, 194.

Jumbles, cocoa-nut, 195.
    plain, 195.
    Spanish, 194.

K.

Kisses, or cream cake, 200

L.

Lady-cake, 211.
Lamb, boiled leg of, 52.
    soup, 18.
    stewed with onions, 52.
Leg of pork, corned and boiled, 55.
Lemonade, 264.
    for an invalid, 241.
Lemon cheese-cake, 124.
    pudding, No. 1, 122.
            No. 2, 123.
    sauce, 101.
    sugared, No. 1, 238.
            No. 2, 239.
    syrup, No. 1, 254.
            No. 2, 254.
Light sugar biscuit, 215.
Lima beans, 98.
Loaf-cake, 189.
    Bristol, 190.
    Indian, 191.
Loaf, Dutch, 207.
    Scotch, 213.
Lobster, boiled, 35.
    salad, 35.

M.

Macaroni, 241.
    265.
Macaroons, 211.
Man oes, pickled, 114.
Marmalade, pea h, 227.
    quince, 227.
Maryland biscuits, 167.
Meats, 36.
Milk biscuits, **177**.
    punch, 267.
    toast, 179.
Minced meat, 258.
Mint julep, 266.

Mint sauce, 106.
Miscellaneous, 254.
Mixture for salting butter, **257**.
Molasses candy, 278.
Muffins, 164.
    Indian, No. 1, 175.
            No. 2, 176.
    Tottenham, 171.
Mulled cider, 239.
    water, 252.
    wine, 239.
Mush bread, 275.
    cakes, 179.
    fried, 266.
    Indian, 265.
Mushrooms, 93.
    catsup, 119.
    pickled, No. 1, 110.
           No. 2, 110.
    sauce, 106.
Mustard, common, 276.
    tomato, 105.
    whey, 245.
Mutton chops, 52.
    with lemon, 53
    dressed like venison, 52.
    tea, 251.

N.

Nasturtiums, pickled, 119.
Newcastle pudding, 141.
New York plum-cake, **185**.
Noodles for soup, 20.
Nuns' butter, 102.
Nuts, dough, 210.
    ginger, 197.

O.

Oatmeal gruel, 242.
Ochras, 94.
Omelette, bread, 261.
    ham, 260.
    oyster, 36.
    plain, 260.
    tomato, 261.
Onion sauce, 106.
    pickled, 111.
    boiled, 97.
    beef stewed with, 41.

INDEX.

Orange fritters, 158.
    cheese-cake, 123.
    jelly, 224.
    pudding, 127.
    sugared, 238.
Orgeat, 235.
Oxford pudding, 148.
Oysters, corn, 90.
    fried, 28.
    pickled, 28.
    scalloped, 29.
    stewed, No. 1, 29.
           No. 2, 29.
    fritters, 30.
    omelette, 31.
        36.
    pie, 30.
    plant, 100.
    sauce, 108.
    soup, 19.

P.

Panada, No. 1, 244.
    No. 2, 244.
Pap of grated flour, 243.
    unbolted flour, 243.
Parsnip cake, 167.
Parsley sauce, 107.
Parsnips, No. 1, 88.
    No. 2, 88.
    No. 3, 88.
    No. 4, 89.
    stewed, 89.
Paste, common, 122.
    plain, 122.
    puff, 121.
Pastry, 120.
Peas green, 99.
Pea soup, 20.
Peach, baked pudding, 142.
    Charlotte, 152.
    dumplings, 136.
    sauce, dried, 102.
    marmalade, 227.
    pie, ripe, 134.
    pot-pie, 135.
Peaches, dried, for pies, 263.
    stewed, ripe, 132.
    pickled, 113.
    preserved, 229.

Pears, baked, 160.
    preserved, 227.
Peppers, pickled, 109.
    pot, 17.
    vinegar, 277.
Pickles, 109.
Pickled beans, 113.
    beets, 117.
    cherries, 117.
    cucumbers, 115.
    eggs, 111.
    mangoes, 114.
    mushrooms, No. 1, 110.
            No. 2, 10.
    nasturtiums, 119.
    onions, 111.
    oysters, 28.
    peaches, 113.
    peppers, 109.
    tomatoes, 120.
    walnuts, 112.
Pie, baked rabbit, 61.
    cherry, 137.
    chicken, 72.
        pot, 73,
    giblet, 71.
    gooseberry, 278.
    green currant, 279.
    oyster, 30.
    peach pot, 135.
    pigeon, 65.
    plain veal, 44.
    plum, 135.
    quince, 135.
    rabbit pot, 62.
    reed-bird, 67.
    rhubarb, 137.
    ripe currant, 279.
    ripe peach, 134.
    veal pot, 45.
Pig's feet, soused, 56.
Pigeon pie, 65.
    roasted, 64.
    stewed, 64.
Pine-apple jam, 233.
    preserved, 228.
Plain apple pudding, No. 3, 130.
    crullers, 286.
    cup-cake, 216.
    fried veal, 48.
    ginger-bread, 199.

Plain jumbles, 195.
   omelette, 260.
   paste, 122.
   veal pie, 44.
Plum cake, New York, 185.
   pies, 135.
   preserved, 232.
   pudding, 145.
Poached eggs, 260.
Pone, Indian, 174.
Pork, leg of, **corned and boiled,** 55.
   steaks, 55.
   stuffed leg of, 55.
Porter sangaree, 259.
Port wine jelly, 247.
Potatoes, boiled, No. **1**, 78.
      No. **2,** 79,
   bread, 274.
   cakes, 81.
   fried, No. **1,** 79.
      No. **2, 80.**
      No. **3, 80.**
      No. **4, 80.**
   jelly, 247.
   kale, 81.
   pudding, 133.
   roasted, 81.
   rolls, 165.
   salad, 82.
   sausage, **83.**
   yeast, 273.
Potted herring, 27.
   shad, No. 1, 25.
      No. 2, 26.
Pound-cake, No. **1,** 186.
      No. 2, 187.
   cocoa-nut, **188.**
   common, 187.
   Indian, 189.
Preserved citron melon, **230.**
   fresh figs, 230.
   green-gages, 231.
   peaches, 229.
   pears, 227.
   pine-apple, **228.**
   plums, 232.
   quinces, 228.
Prunes, stewed, 235.
Pudding, almond, 127.
   apple, No. 1, 129.

Pudding, apple, No. 2, 130.
   arrow-root, for **inva** lids, 236.
   for the **convalescent,** 236.
   baked for invalids, **242.**
      beef and York shire, 59.
   boiled rice, 144.
   cocoa-nut, No. **1,** 128.
      No. 2, 128.
   college, 149.
   Eve's, 138.
   farmers' apple, **142.**
   French, 139.
      bread, **140.**
      custard, **133.**
   green corn, 141.
   Guernsey, 137.
   hasty, or farmers' **rice** 156.
   Indian baked, 147.
      boiled, 146.
   lemon, No. 1, 122.
      No. 2, 123.
   Newcastle, 141.
   orange, 127.
   Oxford, 148.
   peach, baked, 142.
   plain apple, No. **3, 130**.
   potato, 133.
   plum, 145.
   pumpkin, No. **1, 131.**
      No. 2, **131**
   quince, 132.
   rice, with fruit, **144.**
      No. **1,** 143.
      No. 2, 143.
      cup, **141.**
   sago, 139.
      for invalids, 236.
   sweet potato, 134.
   tapioca, 236.
Puffs, German, 158.
   paste, 121.
Pumpkin, dried for pies, **263.**
   pudding, No. 1, 131.
      No. 2, 131.
Punch, 264.
   milk, **267.**

Q.

Queen cake, 288.
Quince dumplings, 136.
    jelly, 226.
    marmalade, 227.
    pie, 135.
    preserved, 228.
    pudding, 132.

R.

Rabbit, French stewed, 63
    fricasseed, 63.
    pot-pie, 62.
    smothered, 64.
Raspberry brandy, 256.
    jam, 233.
    shrub, 257.
    vinegar, 277.
Reed-birds, fried, 67.
    pie, 67.
    roasted, 67.
    stewed, No. 1, 65.
        No. 2, 66.
Rennet, to prepare, 267,
    whey, 246.
Rhubarb pie, 137.
    tarts, 134.
Rice cups, 144.
    cake, 208.
    pudding, 141.
    dumplings, 161.
    florendines, 126.
    flummery, 154.
    ground, No. 1, 245.
        No. 2, 245.
    jelly, 248.
    milk, 153.
    pudding, No. 1, 143.
        No. 2, 143.
        boiled, 144.
        with fruit, 144.
    waffles, 180.
Rich wine sauce, 103.
Ripe currant pie, 279.
    peach pie, 134.
Roast beef, 37.
    chickens, 72.
    duck, No. 1, 69.
        No. 2, 70.

Roast goose, 70.
    leg of lamb, 51.
    oysters, 31.
    pig, 54.
    pigeons, 64.
    pork, 53.
    potatoes, 81.
    rabbit, 61.
    reed-birds, 67.
    turkey, 68.
    veal, 44.
Rock, boiled 21.
    cake, 204.
    fried, 22.
Rolls, Brentford, 166.
    French, 166.
    potato, 165.
Rye batter cakes, 170.
    bread, 275.

S.

Sago pudding, for invalids, 236
        139.
    milk, 234.
Salæratus, to prepare, 264.
Sally Lunn, No. 1, 178.
    No. 2, 178.
Salsify or oyster-plant, No. 1, 100.
        No. 2, 100.
        No. 3, 100.
        No. 4, 101.
Sandwiches, 259.
Sangaree, porter, 259.
    wine, 259.
Sauces, 101.
    caper, 107.
    egg, 105.
    French tomato, 108.
    haslet, 107.
    horse-radish, 109.
    mint, 106.
    mushroom, 106.
    onion, 106.
    oyster, 108.
    parsley, 107.
    tomato, 108.
Sausage meat, 59.
Savoy Charlotte, 152.
Scalloped oysters, 29.
    tomatoes, 84.

Scotch cake, 206,
    crumpets, 172.
    loaf, 213.
Scrapple, 57.
Seed cake, 203.
Shad, baked, 24.
    boiled, 23.
    broiled, 24.
    fried, 24.
    potted, No. 1, 25.
        No. 2, 26.
    roasted on a board, 25.
    to cure, 270.
Shell-fish, 28.
Short-cake, 163.
Shrewsbury cake, 217.
Shrub, currant, 256.
    raspberry, 257.
Slaw, cold, 92.
    French, 92.
    hot, 92.
Slippery-elm tea, 249.
Smothered rabbit, 64.
Smothered steak, 39.
Snow custard, 159.
Soda biscuit, 200.
Soft crabs, 34.
Soup, beef, 15.
    chicken, 18.
    clam, 19.
    corn, 19.
    green corn, 19.
    lamb, 18.
    noodles for, 20.
    oyster, 19.
    pea, 20.
    veal, 16.
    vegetable, 240.
Sour krout, 91.
Soused pig's feet, 56.
Spanish buns, 209.
    fritters, 157.
    jumbles, 194.
Spare rib, 56.
Spiced calves' feet, 49.
    shad, 23.
    veal, 48.
Spinach, 93.
    as greens, 93.
Sponge cake, No. 1, 192.
        No. 2, 193.

Sponge cake, No. 3, 193.
Squashes, or cymlins, 94.
Steak, beef, 38.
Steaks, venison, 60.
Stewed beef's kidney, 41.
    cherries, 160.
    chickens, 75.
    clams, 32.
    oysters, No. 1, 29.
        No. 2, 29.
    ripe peaches, 162.
    pigeons, 64.
    prunes, 235.
    reed-birds, No. 1, 65.
        No. 2, 66.
    sweet-breads, 49.
    tomatoes, 83.
    veal, 47.
Strawberries, glazed, 162.
Strawberry jam, 232.
    jelly, 225.
Stringed beans, 98.
Stuffed leg of pork, 55.
Succotash, 20.
Sugar biscuits, 220.
    light, 215.
    cake, 201.
Sugared lemons, No. 1, 238.
        No. 2, 239.
    orange, 238.
Sweet-breads, boiled, 49.
    for invalids, 243.
    fried, 49.
    stewed, 49.
    dishes, 137.
    potatoes, fried, 80.
        pudding, 134.
Syllabub, 155.
Syrup, lemon, No. 1, 254.
        No. 2, 254.
    ginger, 255.

T.

Tamarind water, 252.
    whey, 247.
Tapioca jelly, 248.
    pudding, 236.
Tarts, cranberry, 134.
    rhubarb, 134.
Tea, 272.

Tea, beef, 250.
    cake, 163.
    chicken, 251.
    flax-seed, 250.
    mutton, 251.
    slippery-elm, 249.
    veal, 250.
Terrapins, 33.
Toast, milk, 179.
    water, 179.
    253.
Tomatoes, baked, 84.
    broiled, 84.
    catsup, No. 1, 117.
        No. 2, 118.
    dressed as cucumbers, 85.
    fricandeau, 85.
    fried, 83.
    mustard, 105.
    omelette, 261.
    pickled, 120.
    sauce, 108.
    scalloped, 84.
    stewed, 83.
Tongue, boiled, 43.
To roast a haunch of venison, 59.
Tottenham muffins, 171.
Travelers' biscuit, 215.
Tripe, 43.
Turkey, boiled, 69.
    roast, 68.
Turnips, 95.

V.

Vanilla cake, 284.
    cup-custards, 156.
Veal, baked fillet of, 46.
    cutlets, 47.
    fillet of, a-la-mode, 46.
    French stew of, 47.
    fried plain, 48.
        with tomatoes, 48.
    pie, plain, 44.
    pot-pie, 45.
    soup, 16

Veal, spiced, 48.
    stewed, 47.
    tea, 250.
Vegetables, 78.
    sauce, 104.
    soup, 240.
Venison, best way of cooking, 60.
    mutton dressed like, 52.
    steaks, 60.
Vinegar celery, 277.
    pepper, 277.
    raspberry, 277
    whey, 246.

W.

Waffles, 168.
    rice, 180.
    without yeast, 169.
Walnut catsup, 119.
    pickled, 112.
Washington cake, No. 1, 218.
        No. 2, 219.
Water toast, 179.
Welsh-rabbit, 266.
Whey, mustard, 245.
    rennet, 246.
    tamarind, 247.
    vinegar, 246.
    wine, 246.
Whips, 155.
White cup-cake, 202.
    fricasseed chicken, 76.
Windsor, or horse beans, 98.
Wine sangaree, 259.
    sauce, 103.
    rich, 103.
    whey, 246.

Y.

Yeast, potato, 273.
    to make, 272.
Yorkshire sauce, 102.
    biscuit, 165.

www.ingramcontent.com/pod-product-compliance
Lightning Source LLC
Chambersburg PA
CBHW030818230426

43667CB00008B/1272